21 世纪英语专业系列教材
国际交流事务系列丛书

English Writing for International Purposes

国际社交文书写作

（英汉双语版）

肖　肃　总主编
张　庆　主编

图书在版编目（CIP）数据

国际社交文书写作：英汉双语版 / 张庆主编. —北京：北京大学出版社，2018.3
（21世纪英语专业系列教材）
ISBN 978-7-301-29017-0

Ⅰ. ①国… Ⅱ. ①张… Ⅲ. ①英语—外交—文书—写作—高等学校—教材
Ⅳ. ①D816

中国版本图书馆CIP数据核字（2017）第303487号

书　　名	国际社交文书写作（英汉双语版） GUOJI SHEJIAO WENSHU XIEZUO (YING-HAN SHUANGYU BAN)
著作责任者	张　庆　主编
责任编辑	刘文静
标准书号	ISBN 978-7-301-29017-0
出版发行	北京大学出版社
地　　址	北京市海淀区成府路205号　100871
网　　址	http://www.pup.cn　　新浪微博：@北京大学出版社
电子信箱	liuwenjing008@163.com
电　　话	邮购部 62752015　发行部 62750672　编辑部 62754382
印 刷 者	北京鑫海金澳胶印有限公司
经 销 者	新华书店
	720毫米×1020毫米　16开本　11.5印张　300千字 2018年3月第1版　2018年3月第1次印刷
定　　价	38.00元

未经许可，不得以任何方式复制或抄袭本书之部分或全部内容。
版权所有，侵权必究
举报电话：010-62752024　电子信箱：fd@pup.pku.edu.cn
图书如有印装质量问题，请与出版部联系，电话：010-62756370

序1

四川外国语大学秉承"外语内核,多元发展"的办学特色定位,一直在积极探索建设适应国家和地方发展需求、服务国家对外开放事业的特色学科专业。我校国际关系学院以提高质量为根本、内涵发展为核心、凝练特色为抓手、适应需求为导向,积极探索融合外交学、国际关系和英语及部分非通用语种等外语专业为一体,培养"国际事务导向,外语与专业能力并重"的复合型人才,实现人才培养"打通学科、按需发展、追求卓越"的目标。

当今世界,中国正在作为一个世界大国和强国崛起,国家的发展对高校人才培养提出了更高、更全面、更多元的要求。对于外语院校而言,过去那种单一专业、单一方向、单一目标、封闭式的人才培养模式已明显不能适应时代的需求。有鉴于此,近年来,我校国际关系学院把培养"厚基础、宽口径、强能力、高素养、复合型"的"大外语"类国际交流型人才作为自己的奋斗目标,大力建设和发展跨外语及其他专业的融合性课程体系和相应师资团队,大力开展国际合作办学,积极推动素质和能力导向的教育教学改革,长期坚持适需对路的教材体系建设,以学生为中心、以学习为重心,为学生倾力打造各种课内、课外学习平台,如外交外事实验教学平台、模拟联合国大会活动、外交风采大赛活动、模拟APEC活动、中外合作办学项目、国际组织人才实验班等等,形成能有力保障教学和学习,富有特色的人才培养平台体系。

"国际交流事务系列丛书"正是在这样的背景下应运而生,是国际关系学院教育教学改革和特色教材建设的重要成果之一。

国际关系学院教师们编写的"国际交流事务系列丛书"是根据这些年教师们课程改革和教学实践的经验,结合国家发展战略和外交外事实践,采用英汉双语模式编写而成的。目前完成编写的有《国际礼仪》《国际会议》《国际公关》《外交谈判》和《国际社交文书写作》等五本教材。这套丛书旨在通过对外交实务的学习和体验,逐步实现业务技能的提升;同时对发展学生的英语能力,特别是专门用途英语能力也十分有帮助。

  由于国际关系学院的人才培养模式还在不断探索和改革中,作为改革的成果,"国际交流事务系列丛书"难免存在一些不足,还需要在改革中不断地完善。但瑕不掩瑜,探索精神难能可贵。

  作为同行和同事,与丛书编写团队共勉——路漫漫其修远兮,吾将上下而求索!

四川外国语大学副校长

王鲁男

序2

中华人民共和国成立初期,周总理对中国外交人员的基本素质提出了"站稳立场、掌握政策、熟悉业务、严守纪律"的十六字方针,成为我国培养外交、外事人才的目标要求。

四川外国语大学国际关系学院年轻教师编写的"国际交流事务系列丛书"无疑践行了十六字方针的内容。丛书体现出来的国际规范、中国特色是站稳立场的表现,形态多样的正反案例是对掌握政策的具体阐释,双语特色是业务能力的一种体现,为此而展开的讨论则体现了学术无禁区、讨论有底线,诠释了外交外事工作的纪律。

《中华人民共和国国民经济和社会发展第十三个五年规划纲要》指出,"如期实现全面建成小康社会奋斗目标,推动经济社会持续健康发展,必须遵循坚持统筹国内国际两个大局。全方位对外开放是发展的必然要求。必须坚持打开国门搞建设,既立足国内,充分运用我国资源、市场、制度等优势,又重视国内国际经济联动效应,积极应对外部环境变化,更好利用两个市场、两种资源,推动互利共赢、共同发展。"当下,举国上下正掀起学习和讨论"十三五"纲要精神的热潮。

笔者曾经先后在外向型企业和高等学校教学一线工作多年,随后转战外交第一线,担任驻外大使、总领事,如今重回高校工作,深感国际事务导向、语言能力并重的国际化人才对于当下中国的意义。国际化人才是事关中华民族伟大复兴,实现"两个一百年"目标的智力资源。"国际交流事务系列丛书"则是中国国际化人才培养上的一次积极尝试,它将为中国的国际化人才培养提供一种新视角。该套丛书着眼于外交事务中的重大事项,通过形态多样的案例来展现外交、外事工作,既有明显的学术性,也有较强的可操作性,不仅易于在校学员学习,也是在职外交、外事人员的有益读物。

欣闻该丛书付梓,是为序。

外交学院党委书记
袁南生

Preface
前　言

随着我国改革开放的不断深入，中外之间的文化交流和商务往来日趋频繁，越来越多的各行各业人士需要接触外部世界。在这纷繁复杂的对外交往中，国际社交文书的应用和写作尤显重要。众多学子走出国门面临各种社会交往任务，这必然要求与之相适应的各种写作指导。可是，近些年来，我国出版了大量应用写作教材、专著，唯独缺少一部囊括学术写作、商务写作和休闲写作在内的著述。这不能不说是一种遗憾。为了适应我国当前改革开放的新形势，满足各界人士在国外学习、工作和生活的需要，我们编写了《国际社交文书写作》。

《国际社交文书写作》收集整理了适用于不同目的与场合的专用写作材料。全书所用材料全部来自国外知名出版社的专业书籍和国外知名高校的写作经验分享，以便让该书的使用者能够充分体验来自国外原汁原味的写作指导，学习并适应国际写作通用惯例。全书共分三部分，分别为学术写作、商务写作、休闲写作。共计13章，覆盖了国际社交文书写作的各个主要应用场合，学术写作包括论文、文献综述和书评、申请书、简历和履历、笔记；商务写作包括备忘录、商务信函和商业报告；休闲写作包括博客和故事写作。该书在编写过程中注意吸收当前最新的理论知识和成果，体例上力求在前人研究的基础上有所创新，每章首先作"内容概览"，概述该类文书的概念、分类、性质、特点、作用和写作要求；"基础知识"部分尽量简明扼要介绍相关背景知识和写作要求；"案例分析"方面，尽量贴近主题，所给示例均为适用于不同场合的经典例文，极具参考价值，分析环节突出重点、析透难点；"拓展阅读"为学生提供与该章内容密切相关的权威中英文阅读材料，并且附上思考练习，促进学生有效吸收消化本章内容；"课后练习"选材精炼、针对性强，能达到让学生举一反三、灵活运用的目的。另外，根据文书写作必须具备的实用性的特点，在练习中增加了情景模拟环节，引导学生通过各种虚拟场景了解和掌握各章内容，以便能在写作时游刃有余,恰到好处地处理各种不同类型的写作实践。

本书有利于扩大学习者的英语词汇量,增强用英语撰写的基本能力,提高学习者的英文水平;简单易懂的基础理论搭配形式多样的案例,有助于训练读者思辨能力和案例分析能力;题型丰富的课后练习可以进一步夯实学习者的基础知识,培养多元化的写作技能技巧。该书具有以下几个方面的突出特点:

▶ 语言的实用性。为适应国际交流的客观需求,全书力求用中英文双语讲解。所选取的案例、拓展阅读材料以及课后练习均以英语为主,以培养学生灵活运用两种语言的能力。

▶ 取材的广泛性。适用于不同场合的论文、申请书、备忘录和主要商务信函,以及与之相应的写作技巧、方法和参考范例等都可以在书中找到。书中列举了大量具有实践意义的经典案例。

▶ 内容的现代性。书中所编撰的内容尽量与现实紧密结合,范例大多是目前实际生活中正在运用的,尤其是在我国不断融入国际进程,与国际政治经济接轨后的写作技巧与范例。

《国际社交文书写作》是在四川外国语大学国际关系学院的通盘统筹和具体策划下编写的,自始至终离不开出版社同志的关照和指导,在该书付梓之际,谨向他们表示深深的谢意。在本书编写过程中,来自重庆外国语学校的龙凌老师为本书的构思立意、章节安排和体例排版提出了中肯的建议,来自四川外国语大学国际关系学院的聂巧仪、赵鑫、代小艳、李伊璇和谭欣贻几位同学在资料搜集、整理和校对方面给予了巨大支持。在此感谢他们付出的辛勤劳动。

在编写过程中,我们参考借鉴了国内外有关教材和研究成果、网络资料,吸取了其中许多有益的内容,在此不一一列举,谨向有关作者表示深切的谢意。尽管付出了极大的努力,但由于我们水平有限、时间仓促,这其中肯定会有这样那样的不足,万望同仁和专家批评指正,以便进一步修改完善。

张　庆

2017 年 10 月

Contents
目　录

Part One　Academic Writing
第一部分　学术写作

Chapter 1　Academic Writing Style / 学术写作概述

Abstract ／内容概览 ·· 3
The Purposes of Academic Writing ／学术写作的目的 ················ 4
The Requirements of Academic Writing ／学术写作要求 ·············· 6
Exercise ／课后练习 ··· 9

Chapter 2　Essay / 论文

Abstract ／内容概览 ·· 11
Basic Knowledge ／基础知识 ······································· 12
Case Studies ／案例分析 ··· 17
Supplementary Readings ／拓展阅读 ································ 20
Exercise ／课后练习 ·· 21

Chapter 3　Literature Review and Book Review / 文献综述和书评

Abstract ／内容概览 ·· 23

Section 1　Literature Review ／文献综述 ··························· 24
Basic Knowledge ／基础知识 ······································· 24
Case Studies ／案例分析 ··· 25

1

Supplementary Readings ／拓展阅读 ·· 27

Section 2　Book Review ／书评 ·· 29
Basic Knowledge ／基础知识 ··· 29
Case Studies ／案例分析 ·· 32
Supplementary Readings ／拓展阅读 ·· 34
Exercise ／课后练习 ·· 35

Chapter 4　Application Essay / 申请书

Abstract ／内容概览 ·· 36
Basic Knowledge ／基础知识 ··· 37
Case Studies ／案例分析 ·· 41
Supplementary Readings ／拓展阅读 ·· 44
Exercise ／课后练习 ·· 46

Chapter 5　Resume and CV / 简历和履历

Abstract ／内容概览 ·· 48

Section 1　Resume ／简历 ·· 49
Basic Knowledge ／基础知识 ··· 49
Case Studies ／案例分析 ·· 51
Supplementary Readings ／拓展阅读 ·· 53

Section 2　CV ／履历 ·· 56
Basic Knowledge ／基础知识 ··· 56
Case Studies ／案例分析 ·· 63
Supplementary Readings ／拓展阅读 ·· 67
Exercise ／课后练习 ·· 69

Chapter 6 Note Making / 笔记

Abstract ／ 内容概览 ·· 71
Basic Knowledge ／ 基础知识 ·· 71
Case Studies ／ 案例分析 ·· 75
Supplementary Readings ／ 拓展阅读 ··· 76
Exercise ／ 课后练习 ·· 78

Part Two Business Writing
第二部分　商务写作

Chapter 7 Business Writing Style / 商务写作概述

Abstract ／ 内容概览 ·· 83
The Purposes of Business Writing ／ 商业写作目的 ······················· 83
The Requirements of Business Writing ／ 商务写作要求 ················ 85
Exercise ／ 课后练习 ·· 88

Chapter 8 Memo / 备忘录

Abstract ／ 内容概览 ·· 90
Basic Knowledge ／ 基础知识 ·· 91
Case Studies ／ 案例分析 ·· 98
Supplementary Readings ／ 拓展阅读 ·· 101
Exercise ／ 课后练习 ·· 103

Chapter 9 Business Letters / 商务信函

Abstract ／ 内容概览 ·· 104
Basic Knowledge ／ 基础知识 ·· 105
Case Studies ／ 案例分析 ·· 111
Supplementary Readings ／ 拓展阅读 ·· 116
Exercise ／ 课后练习 ·· 118

Chapter 10　Business Report / 商业报告

Abstract ／内容概览 ··· 119
Basic Knowledge ／基础知识 ·· 120
Case Studies ／案例分析 ·· 124
Supplementary Readings ／拓展阅读 ································· 127
Exercise ／课后练习 ·· 130

Part Three　Leisure Writing
第三部分　休闲写作

Chapter 11　Leisure Writing Style / 休闲写作概述

Abstract ／内容概览 ··· 133
The Purposes of Leisure Writing ／休闲写作目的 ····················· 134
The Requirements of Leisure Writing ／休闲写作要求 ················· 135
Exercise ／课后练习 ·· 137

Chapter 12　Blog Writing / 博客写作

Abstract ／内容概览 ··· 139
Basic Knowledge ／基础知识 ·· 140
Case Studies ／案例分析 ·· 143
Supplementary Readings ／拓展阅读 ································· 144
Exercise ／课后练习 ·· 145

Chapter 13　Short Story / 故事写作

Abstract ／内容概览 ··· 146
Basic Knowledge ／基础知识 ·· 147
Case Studies ／案例分析 ·· 152
Supplementary Readings ／拓展阅读 ································· 154
Exercise ／课后练习 ·· 157

Keys／参考答案 ·· **158**

References／参考文献 ·· **166**

Part One　Academic Writing

第一部分　学术写作

Chapter 1

Academic Writing Style
学术写作概述

Academic writing refers to a style of expression that researchers use to define the intellectual boundaries of their disciplines and their specific areas of expertise. Characteristics of academic writing include a formal tone, use of the third-person rather than first-person perspective (usually), a clear focus on the research problem under investigation, and precise word choice. Like specialist languages adopted in other professions, such as, law or medicine, academic writing is designed to convey agreed meaning about complex ideas or concepts for a group of scholarly experts.[1]

Academic writing has always played a large and central role for students all over the world. School and university teachers spend many weeks of the year trying to pass on their knowledge and teach their students to write academically, as they know the benefits of acquiring this skill early on.

学术写作指的是研究人员用来定义他们学科的知识边界和特定领域的专业术语的一种表达方式。学术写作的特点包括正式的语气、第三人称的使用而不是第一人称的视角（大部分情况下）、明确关注研究中的问题以及精确的用词。如同法律或医学行业采用特定的专业语言，学术写作旨在由学术专家传达关于复杂思想或概念的约定意义。

对于世界各地的学生来说，学术写作在其学习生涯中一直扮演着重要角色。学校和大学教师花费了大量时间，试图通过传播相关知识来教会学生如何进行学术写作，因为他们清楚地知道尽早获得这项技能的好处。

---

[1] James Hartley, *Academic Writing and Publishing: A Practical Guide*. New York: Routledge, 2008.

The Purposes of Academic Writing
学术写作的目的

1. It teaches students to analyze

Academic writing usually requires students to look at somebody else's work or ideas and then form an informed opinion on it. Instead of merely describing the work of other people, students have to think about why it has been carried out and which uses its findings may have for the future. This type of writing makes students take in what they have read and decide how much importance it holds for their subject.

2. It allows students to convey their understanding

When students learn about a complex subject at university, it can be difficult for them to explain what they have understood if they struggle with academic writing. Essays give students the chance to explain what they have learnt by using the correct terminology and styles to make the information understood by others.

3. It has a strong focus on technique and style

Unlike some less formal types of writing, academic writing focuses on technique and how it should be used to best convey ideas. If students learn about style and how to write essays early on in their academic careers, they will find it much easier to write papers throughout university. Many lecturers have preferred styles or formatting requirements, so academic writing forces students to take these into consideration and create a paper that will impress. It is usually a good idea for students to ask for essay writing help if they are having issues with their technique, as this is something that can be solved with a little guidance.

4. It teaches students to think critically and objectively

Students should never write a one-sided paper that leaves no room for argument. Academic writing forces them to look at ideas and research from a different perspective, as this is what they will need to do in order to obtain good grades. Students have to learn to analyze theories from a number of different viewpoints and then make statements based on what they understand. This is an extremely useful skill for people to learn early on in life, as the ability to look at things objectively is something that will benefit them in real life.①

1. 教会学生如何去分析

学术写作通常要求学生去阅读别人的作品或了解其想法，然后形成一个有见地的观点。不应仅仅描述其他人的作品，学生们还得思考它是怎么产生的，而它的发现可能会对未来产生影响。这种类型的写作使得学生们理解了他们所读到的内容，并决定了他们对主题的重视程度。

2. 允许学生表达个人理解

当学生们在大学里学习一门复杂的课程时，如果他们感到学术写作很困难，那么他们很难解释此前所理解的内容。学术论文则让学生有机会用正确的术语和风格来解释他们所学到的知识，从而使这些信息被他人理解。

3. 注重技巧与风格

与一些不太正式的写作类型不同，学术写作侧重于写作技巧，以及如何用它来最好地传达思想。如果学生在学习生涯的早期就学习了论文写作方法，他们会发现在大学里写论文变得更容易了。许多老师都有自己喜欢的风格或格式要求，所以学术写作迫使学生们把这些因素考虑进去，并创作一篇将会给人留下深刻印象的论文。通常学生在技巧上遇到的问题，可以通过写作指导来有效解决的。

4. 教会学生客观地、批判性地思考

学生不应该写一篇没有任何争论余地的片面文章。学术写作要求他们从不同的角度去看待想法和研究，这是他们为了取得好成绩所必须做的事情。学生必须学会从不同的观点分析理论，然后根据他们的理解做出陈述。这是一种非常有用的技能，最好尽早学习，因为客观看待事物的能力在现实生活中会使人们受益。

---

① https://ewritingservice.com/blog/what-is-the-importance-of-academic-writing-for-a-student/

The Requirements of Academic Writing
学术写作要求

Avoid some aspects of informal English

- Don't (do not!) use contractions (e.g. it's, he'll, it'd etc.): always use the full form (it is/has, he will, it would/had).
- Don't use colloquial language or slang (e.g. kid, a lot of/lots of, cool)
- Always write as concisely as you can, with no irrelevant material or "waffle".
- Generally avoid "phrasal verbs" (e.g. get off, get away with, put in etc): instead, use one word equivalents.
- Avoid common but vague words and phrases such as get, nice, thing. Your writing needs to be more precise.
- Avoid overuse of brackets; don't use exclamation marks or dashes; avoid direct questions; don't use "etc".
- Always use capital letters appropriately and never use the type of language used in texting!

Structure your writing carefully

- Make sure you write in complete sentences.
- Divide your writing up into paragraphs.
- Use connecting words and phrases to make your writing explicit and easy to follow.
- Check your grammar and spelling carefully.

Make your writing formal and impersonal

- Avoid too much personal language (I, my, we etc.). Some tutors prefer you to avoid it completely. Never use emotive language; be objective rather than subjective.
- Avoid being too dogmatic and making sweeping generalizations. It is usually best to use some sort of "hedging" language and to qualify statements that you make.
- You should consistently use evidence from your source reading to back up what you are saying and reference this correctly.

- Avoid sexist language, such as chairman, mankind. Don't refer to "the doctor" as he; instead, make the subject plural and refer to them as they. Avoid he/she, herself/himself etc.
- Use nominalization; that is, try to write noun-based phrases rather that verb-based ones.

  For example, instead of
  Crime was increasing rapidly and the police were becoming concerned.
  Write:
  The rapid increase in crime was causing concern among the police.

  In general, academic writing tends to be fairly dense, with relatively long sentences and wide use of subordinate clauses. Remember, however, that your main aim is clarity, so don't be too ambitious, particularly when you're starting to write.

Hedging/Avoiding commitment

  In order to put some distance between what you're writing and yourself as writer, to be cautious rather than assertive, you should:

- Avoid overuse of first person pronouns (I, we, my, our)
- Use impersonal subjects instead (It is believed that ..., it can be argued that ...)
- Use passive verbs to avoid stating the "doer" (Tests have been conducted)
- Use verbs (often with it as subject) such as imagine, suggest, claim, suppose
- Use "attitudinal signals" such as apparently, arguably, ideally, strangely, unexpectedly.
- These words allow you to hint at your attitude to something without using personal language.
- Use verbs such as would, could, may, might which "soften" what you're saying.
- Use qualifying adverbs such as some, several, a minority of, a few, many to avoid making overgeneralizations.①

避免在某些方面使用非正式英语

1. 不要使用缩写，如 it's, he'll, it'd 等。始终使用完整的拼写形式，如 it is/has,

---

① Study Guides: Writing, Center for Academic Success, Birmingham City University, http://library.bcu.ac.uk/learner/writingguides/1. 20. htm

he will, it would/had。
2. 不要使用俗语或俚语，如 kid, a lot of/lots of, cool。
3. 尽可能行文简洁，不要使用无关紧要的材料或"胡扯闲聊"。
4. 通常避免"动词短语"，如 get off, get away with, put in 等，而以单词代之。
5. 避免常见但含糊的词和短语，例如 get, nice, thing。用词需要更加准确。
6. 避免过度使用括号；不要使用感叹号或破折号；避免直接疑问句；不要用"etc"。
7. 始终正确使用大写字母，绝对不要使用发短信的语言类型！

谨慎组织文章

1. 一定要使用完整的语言。
2. 把文章分成段落。
3. 使用连接词和短语使你的文章清晰易懂。
4. 仔细检查文章语法和拼写。

让你的文章正式且客观

1. 避免过多的个人语言（如 I, my, we etc.）。不要使用情绪化的语言；用语得客观，不能太过于主观化。
2. 避免过于教条和笼统的概括。通常最好使用某种"模糊"语言，并使之符合你的陈述。
3. 你应该始终正确引用你所陈述的内容，做到有据可查。
4. 避免性别歧视的语言，比如 Chairman, mankind。不要称呼"the Doctor"为 he；相反，把主语变成复数。避免使用 he/she, herself/himself, 诸如此类。
5. 使用名词化结构；也就是说，试着写出基于名词的短语，而不是基于动词的短语。

举个例子，不要使用

Crime was increasing rapidly and the police were becoming concerned.

而用

The rapid increase in crime was causing concern among the police.

一般来说，学术写作句子相对较长，从属分句广泛使用。但是，请记住，你的主要目标是追求清楚明了，尤其是当你初学写作的时候，不要过于雄心勃勃。

模糊/避免承诺

为了谨慎行文而不是武断用词，你应该：
1. 避免过度使用第一人称代词（I, we, my, our）。
2. 使用客观对象（It is believed that ..., it can be argued that ...）。
3. 使用被动语态来避免说出行为的实施者（Tests have been conducted）。
4. 使用动词（通常跟随其主语），如 imagine, suggest, claim, suppose。
5. 使用"表现态度的信号"，如 apparently, arguably, ideally, strangely, unexpectedly。这些话可以让你在不使用个人语言的情况下暗示你对某事的态度。
6. 使用如 would, could, may, might 的动词可弱化语气。
7. 使用一些如 some, several, a minority of, a few, many 的副词来避免过分概括。

Exercise 课后练习

● **True or False**

Directions: Read the following sentences and decide whether they are true or false.

1. Do not use contractions in your academic writing, always use the full form.
2. You can use "kid" in your academic writing.
3. Never use the type of language used in texting in your academic writing.

● **Gap-Filling**

Directions: Complete each sentence with appropriate words.

1. Avoid _____, such as chairman, mankind.
2. Use _____ to avoid stating the "_____".
3. Use _____ such as some, several, a minority of, a few, many to avoid making _____.

● **Short Answer Questions**

Directions: Answer the following questions briefly.

1. What are the purposes of academic writing?
2. What should you do when you want to avoid stating the "doer"?

● **Simulative Exercise**

Suppose you are invited to share some tips of academic writing with your classmates, what should you say to them?

Chapter 2

Essay
论文

Abstract
内容概览

Essay is a commonly assigned form of writing that every student will encounter while in academia. It often involves constructing a debate around a particular issue, comparing two or more related ideas, or persuading readers of a particular argument or position. Therefore, it is wise for student to become capable and comfortable with this type of writing early on in their training.

Essays can be a rewarding and challenging type of writing and are often assigned either to be done in class, which requires previous planning and practice (and a bit of creativity) on the part of the student, or as homework, which likewise demands a certain amount of preparation. Many poorly crafted essays have been produced on account of a lack of preparation and confidence. However, students can avoid the discomfort often associated with essay writing by understanding some common features of essay writing.

论文是一种常见的写作形式，每一位进行学术研究的学生都将接触到这类写作。它通常涉及围绕某一特定问题展开辩论，对两个或多个相互联系的想法进行对比，或是说服读者信服某一特定的论点或立场。因此，学生在早期训练阶段就学会并适应这一类写作是明智之选。

论文这一写作类型既会使人受益匪浅，同时也兼具挑战性。有时，它属于需要当堂完成的任务。在这种情况下，学生需要提前做好计划及练习（也要求一定创造力）。论文也会是课下作业，此时，学生同样要进行一定程度的准备。由于缺乏准备和自信，很多同学会写出拙劣的文章。同学们可以通过理解论文写作的几点共性特征来避免写作过程中的不适感。

Basic Knowledge
基础知识

Introduction

Essays are one of the hardest assignment tasks to get a handle on. They require more than presenting what has happened in a field of work. Typically, they involve you constructing a debate around the different arguments in favour of or not in favour of a particular issue.

It is often a good idea to imagine yourself as a lawyer when thinking about how you are going to write your essay. As a lawyer, you have to be able to persuade and convince the jury of your point of view, while also acknowledging the opposition's arguments, but then downplaying them in some way by mentioning their weaknesses or disadvantages. By highlighting the weaknesses in arguments that oppose your point of view, this functions to strengthen the merits of your argument.

It is always good to be aware of alternative views, interpretations, and evidence surrounding an assignment topic and to acknowledge them in your assignment. However, this does not necessarily mean that you have to agree with these views. At least, by mentioning them you show the marker that you have read widely, you are well informed on the issue, and you are not biased in your position.

简介

论文是最难处理的写作任务之一。它要求的不单单是你要将一个领域中所发生的事情呈现出来。通常情况下，论文要求写作者围绕自己对某一特定问题所持的赞成或反对的观点进行论述。

在你思考如何撰写自己的论文时，最好将自己设想成一位律师。作为律师，你必须能够让陪审团信服你的观点，同时也承认反对派的论点，但随后以某种方式指出这些观点的不足或劣势。强调对立观点的缺陷会有助于强化你的论点。

对于此类写作非常有帮助的一点是，要做到时刻熟知与指定话题有关的各种观点、解释方式和例证，并且要在论文写作中运用它们。虽然不要求你必须同意这些观点，但谈及这些内容将会显示出你广泛的阅读面、你对这个问题有充分的了解以及没有偏见的立场。

Writing Requirement

1. Planning

It is really important to plan your essay before you begin writing. Planning will save you time later. It is also essential that you have a starting point to plan from, even if it is in a very rough form.

The obvious place to start is at the assignment question itself. From the question you can develop your answer in the form of a thesis statement. From there you can decide what your essay's subtopics will be and what you want to say about them. After you have a basic idea of what you want to talk about, you can begin to write the essay.

However, when writing an essay, it can also be difficult to come up with a point of view early on. Therefore, instead of developing a thesis statement first, you may choose to read up on the assignment question and make notes on relevant concepts, theories, and studies. Once you have these notes and can develop a summary of the issues, it should be much easier to write a thesis statement.

2. Structuring

All essays share the same basic structure, although they may differ in content and style. The essence of an essay is an opinion, expressed as a thesis statement or proposition, and a logical sequence of arguments and information organized in support of the proposition.

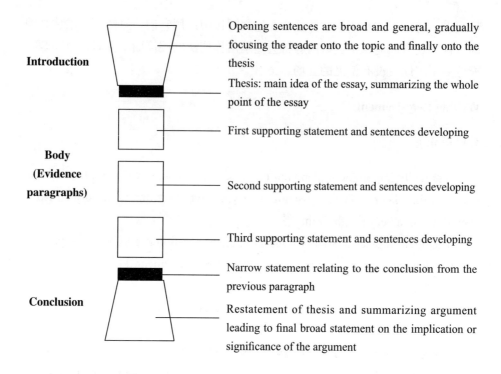

3. Essay Revision

Before you submit your essay for marking, you should have another look over it and improve it wherever possible.

The most important question is this: have I answered the question? Return to your original interpretation of the assignment question and check it against your final answer.

You may also be too far above or below the word limit. See word limits and assignment length for actions you can take in this situation.

At this stage you should review the content of the essay:
- Are there any unexplained contradictions?
- Can anything be written more clearly?
- Are the main ideas easy to identify?

Some other important revision questions for essays relate to the structure and flow:
- Does the introduction contain a clear thesis statement?
- Does each body paragraph have a unique topic sentence?

- Does the essay flow within paragraphs and between paragraphs?
- Have the main points of the argument been summarized in the conclusion?

Look over your use of outside sources:

- Are quotations relevant, accurate, and integrated into the paragraphs?
- Is all paraphrased material used correctly and integrated into the paragraphs?
- Are all outside sources referenced correctly?
- Is there a reference list?[①]

写作要求

1. 计划

在开始写作之前，计划好你的论文非常重要。事先计划会为你之后的工作节省很多时间。即使是以非常粗糙的形式，你也要有一个可以开始计划的起点。

写作任务本身所包含的问题就是一个显而易见的起点。从这个问题出发，你可以写出中心句，进而展开你的回答。在此基础上，你可以决定论文的副标题以及内容。在对于内容有了基本把握之后，你就可以开始写作了。

但是人们很难在写文章的初期就想出一个观点。所以在点明主旨之前，你最好先熟读写作任务中的问题要求，阅读相关的概念、理论以及研究调查，并做好笔记。一旦你做到上述要求，并能对议题进行概括总结，写中心句就会轻松很多。

2. 列框架

尽管不同论文的内容与风格不同，它们的基本结构都是一样的。一篇论文的核心要素就是作者的观点。它通常以文章的中心思想或是中心命题呈现出来。另一个核心要素是文章的逻辑顺序，其中涵盖着支撑命题的论据及信息。

---

① http://owll.massey.ac.nz/assignment-types/essay-revision.php

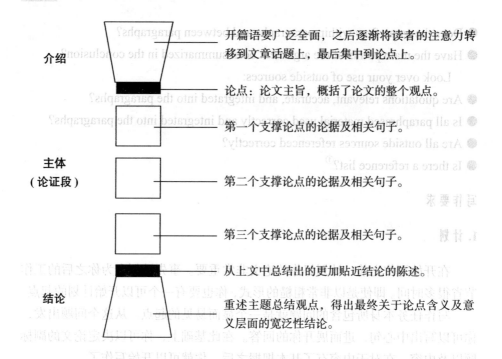

3. 修订论文

你应该在提交之前再次检查并尽可能地完善你的论文。

问自己一个最为重要的的问题：我回答清楚这个问题了吗？回到最开始写作任务中的问题，再对照检查自己最终给出的答案是否回答了该问题。

你有可能超出或是低于字数限制。你需要考虑单词字数及文章的篇幅限定，并且进行修订。

在此阶段，你应该回顾一下论文的内容：
- 文章中是否存在无法解释、前后矛盾的内容？
- 内容的表述是否可以更清晰一些？
- 中心思想是否明晰？

在修订过程中，还有一些有关结构与文章发展的问题需要特别注意：
- 简介中是否含有一个清晰的中心论点？
- 是否每一个主体段落都包含其独有的主题句？
- 整篇文章及各段落间是否均自然过渡？
- 结尾段中是否总结了各个主要分论点？

检查对外部资源的引用：
- 引用是否相关、精确、并融入段落？
- 所有的释义运用是否正确？是否能够融入段落？
- 是否所有对外部资源的引用都正确？
- 文后是否列出了参考文献？

Case Studies 案例分析

As people rely more and more on technology to solve problems, the ability of humans to think for themselves will surely deteriorate. Discuss the extent to which you agree or disagree with the statement and explain your reasoning for the position you take. In developing and supporting your position, you should consider ways in which the statement might or might not hold true and explain how these considerations shape your position.

The statement linking technology negatively with free thinking plays on recent human experience over the past century. Surely there has been no time in history when the lived lives of people have changed more dramatically. A quick reflection on a typical day reveals how technology has revolutionized the world. Most people commute to work in an automobile that runs on an internal combustion engine. During the workday, chances are high that the employee will interact with a computer that processes information on silicon bridges that are .09 microns wide. Upon leaving home, family members will be reached through wireless networks that utilize satellites orbiting the earth. Each of these common occurrences could have been inconceivable at the turn of the 19th century.

The statement attempts to bridge these dramatic changes to a reduction in the ability for humans to think for themselves. The assumption is that an increased reliance on technology negates the need for people to think creatively to solve previous quandaries. Looking back at the introduction, one could argue that without a car, computer, or mobile phone, the hypothetical worker would need to find alternate methods of transport, information processing and communication. Technology short circuits this thinking by making the problems obsolete.

However, this reliance on technology does not necessarily preclude the creativity that marks the human species. The prior examples reveal that technology allows for convenience. The car, computer and phone all release additional time for people to live more efficiently. This efficiency does not preclude the need for humans to think for themselves. In fact, technology frees humanity to not only tackle new problems, but may itself create new issues that did not exist without technology. For example, the proliferation of automobiles has introduced a need for fuel conservation on a global scale. With increasing energy demands from emerging markets, global warming becomes a concern inconceivable to the horse-and-buggy generation. Likewise dependence on oil has created nation-states that are not dependent on taxation, allowing ruling parties to oppress minority groups such as women. Solutions to these complex problems require the unfettered imaginations of maverick scientists and politicians.

In contrast to the statement, we can even see how technology frees the human imagination. Consider how the digital revolution and the advent of the internet has allowed for an unprecedented exchange of ideas. WebMD, a popular internet portal for medical information, permits patients to self research symptoms for a more informed doctor visit. This exercise opens pathways of thinking that were previously closed off to the medical layman. With increased interdisciplinary interactions, inspiration can arrive from the most surprising corners. Jeffrey Sachs, one of the architects of the UN Millennium Development Goals, based his ideas on emergency care triage techniques. The unlikely marriage of economics and medicine has healed tense, hyperinflation environments from South America to Eastern Europe.

This last example provides the most hope in how technology actually provides hope to the future of humanity. By increasing our reliance on technology, impossible goals can now be achieved. Consider how the late 20th century witnessed the complete elimination of smallpox. This disease had ravaged the human race since prehistorical days, and yet with the technology of vaccines, free thinking humans dared to imagine a world free of smallpox.

> Using technology, battle plans were drawn out, and smallpox was systematically targeted and eradicated.
>
> Technology will always mark the human experience, from the discovery of fire to the implementation of nanotechnology. Given the history of the human race, there will be no limit to the number of problems, both new and old, for us to tackle. There is no need to retreat to a Luddite attitude to new things, but rather embrace a hopeful posture to the possibilities that technology provides for new avenues of human imagination.

（文献来源：http://www. ets. org/gre/revised_general/prepare/analytical_writing/issue/sample_responses）

Analysis

The author of this essay stakes out a clear and insightful position on the issue and follows the specific instructions by presenting reasons to support that position. The essay cogently argues that technology does not decrease our ability to think for ourselves, but merely provides additional time for people to live more efficiently." In fact, the problems that have developed alongside the growth of technology (pollution, political unrest in oil-producing nations) actually call for more creative thinking, not less.

In further examples, the essay shows how technology allows for the linking of ideas that may never have been connected in the past (like medicine and economic models), pushing people to think in new ways. Examples are persuasive and fully developed; reasoning is logically sound and well supported.

Ideas in the essay are connected logically, with effective transitions used both between paragraphs ("However" or "In contrast to the statement") and within paragraphs. Sentence structure is varied and complex and the essay clearly demonstrates facility with the "conventions of standard written English" (i.e. , grammar, usage and mechanics), with only minor errors appearing. Thus, this essay meets all the requirements for receiving a top score.

Supplementary Readings
拓展阅读

As you reflect on life thus far, what has someone said, written, or expressed in some fashion that is especially meaningful to you. Why?

According to Mother Teresa, "If you judge someone, you have no time to love them". I first saw this quote when it was posted on my sixth-grade classroom wall, and I hated it. Rather, I hated Mother Teresa's intention, but I knew that the quote's veracity was inarguable. I felt that it was better to judge people so as not to have to love them, because some people don't deserve a chance. Judgments are shields, and mine was impenetrable.

Laura was my dad's first girlfriend after my parents' divorce. The first three years of our relationship were characterized solely by my hatred toward her, manifested in my hurting her, each moment hurting myself twice as much. From the moment I laid eyes on her, she was the object of my unabated hatred, not because of anything she had ever done, but because of everything she represented. I judged her to be a heartless, soulless, two-dimensional figure: she was a representation of my loneliness and pain. I left whenever she entered a room, I slammed car doors in her face. Over those three years, I took pride in the fact that I had not spoken a word to her or made eye contact with her. I treated Laura with such resentment and anger because my hate was my protection, my shield. I, accustomed to viewing her as the embodiment of my pain, was afraid to let go of the anger and hate, afraid to love the person who allowed me to hold onto my anger, afraid that if I gave her a chance, I might love her.

For those three years, Laura didn't hate me; she understood me. She understood my anger and my confusion, and Laura put her faith in me, although she had every reason not to. To her, I was essentially a good person, just confused and scared; trying to do her best, but just not able to get a hold of herself. She saw me as I wished I could see myself.

None of this became clear to me overnight. Instead, over the next two years, the one-dimensional image of her in my mind began to take the shape of a person. As I let go of my hatred, I gave her a chance. She became a woman who, like me, loves Ally McBeal and drinks a lot of coffee; who, unlike me, buys things advertised on infomercials.

　　Three weeks ago, I saw that same Mother Teresa quote again, but this time I smiled. Laura never gave up on me, and the chance she gave me to like her was a chance that changed my life. Because of this, I know the value of a chance, of having faith in a person, of seeing others as they wish they could see themselves. I'm glad I have a lot of time left, because I definitely have a lot of chances left to give, a lot of people left to love.

（文献来源：http://www. studymode. com/essays/Mother-Teresa-38974231. html）

Reading Comprehension

1. What does the quote of Mother Teresa mean?
2. Why did the author treat Laura with anger?
3. What is the function of telling the story of "me" and Laura?
4. Does the author still hate the quote now?

Exercise 课后练习

● **True or False**

Directions: Read the following sentences and decide whether they are true or false.

1. Essays that are assigned to be done in class only require a bit of creativity.
2. Before developing a thesis statement, you should develop the structure of the essay.
3. All essays share the same basic structure.

● **Gap-Filling**

Directions: Complete each sentence with appropriate words.

1. It is often a good idea to imagine yourself as a _____ when thinking about how you are going to write your essay. As a lawyer, you have to be able to _____ and _____ the jury of your point of view.

2. The essence of an essay is an _____, expressed as a thesis statement or proposition, and a _____ sequence of arguments and information organized in support of the proposition.

● **Short Answer Questions**

Directions: Answer the following questions briefly.

1. What you should do before developing a thesis statement?
2. What is the key to the review of the essay?

● **Simulative Exercise**

　　Based on your understanding of requirements and methods of essay writing, choose a issue related to your major and write a essay about it.

Literature Review and Book Review
文献综述和书评

Abstract
内容概览

Literature reviews provide a critical overview of a range of sources (literature) on a particular topic. They are sections of a paper in which the writer summarizes recently published work on the topic. This is often done in the context of a larger study, to provide a solid foundation for further research. In most papers a summary of relevant and recent authorities is included in the introduction.

A book review is a critical assessment of a book. It describes and evaluates the quality and significance of a book and does not merely summarize the content. Book reviews are frequently written by publishers, editors and newspaper and journal reviewers as part of the publicity process for a book shortly after publication or republication. They are also written by experts, academics, journalists, organizations with vested interests and students to develop an understanding of the place of a particular book within a broader context of its subject area and its genre.

文献综述是围绕某一特定主题就一系列相关文献资料而进行的批判性的评论。它通常是在作者总结与主题相关的近期出版物的基础上完成,属于论文的一部分,目的是为更深入的研究提供坚实的基础。在论文中,通常文献综述置于介绍部分。

书评是对一本书进行批判性的评定。它旨在描述和估量书的质量和价值,而不仅仅是总结内容。书评作为书籍出版或再版后提高其知名度的一个过程,通常由出版者、编辑和报纸杂志评论家来撰写。此外,书评的作者也可由专家、学者、记者、相关组织以及学生充当,目的在于在一个更为宏观的语境下增进对一本书所占有地位的理解。

Section 1 | Literature Review 文献综述

Basic Knowledge 基础知识

Introduction

The key to the review of the literature is not to provide a shopping list of past papers. Instead your aim is to state:

1. what others have done or what you did in a previous paper;

2. the downside or limit of what they did or why you decided to further the work you did in a previous paper;

3. your solution and improvement.

简介

文献综述的核心并不在于提供过往文献资料的清单,而在于以下几点:

1. 其他人或你自己以前在相关领域做了什么研究;

2. 前人研究成果的缺陷,为什么你决定在以前的基础上继续深入这项研究;

3. 你的解决方案或改进方案是什么。

Writing Requirement

Occasionally, the whole focus of an essay may be a lengthy literature review, but in most student writing it will only form a relatively short section of the paper. Only a minority have a separate section headed "The Literature" or "Literature Review". In all cases, it is necessary to show that you are familiar with the main sources, so that your writing can build on these.

A literature review is not simply a list of sources that you have studied. It can be used to show that there is a gap in the research that your work attempts to fill:

This article has a different standpoint from other studies, because it believes that the influence of the state on the market has structurally increased since the neo-

liberal era.

This article focuses on information production, not information accessibility. That is the difference between this research and previous studies ...

It is also common to use the literature section to clarify the varying positions held by other researchers:

The political competition literature comprises two main strands—voter monitoring and political survival.

Writers may also show how changes in thought have appeared at different times:

Of late, a number of papers (Besley et al., 2006; Besley and Preston, 2007; Persson and Tabellini, 2000) have collated the various arguments ...

写作要求

少数文章会将全文焦点放在详尽的文献综述上。对于大多数学生写作而言，文献综述仅是文章的一个部分而已。有时这个部分会以"研究综述"或"文献综述"的标题单独列出。这个部分有必要展现出你对相关资料的熟悉程度，以便在此基础上进行更深入的研究。

文献综述不仅仅是你研究的资料清单，而应说明现有研究的缺陷以及你的目的在于填补这些缺陷，如：

本文的观点有别于其他研究，认为自从进入新自由主义时代，国家对市场的影响力有了结构性的增强。

本文聚焦于信息生产，而非信息获取，这是该项研究与先前研究的区别……

文献综述的另一个目的在于厘清其他研究者的不同立场和观点，如：
有关政治竞争的文献主要由两部分组成——投票者监督和政治生存。

此外，文献综述需要指出不同时期的观点演变，如：

最近，很多文章 (Besley et al., 2006; Besley and Preston, 2007; Persson and Tabellini, 2000) 都梳理了不同的观点……

Case Studies 案例分析

Below is an extract from the Introduction to a paper entitled The Effects of

Feedback and Attribution Style on Task Persistence where psychology student Chris Rozek begins his review of the literature.

> Persistence has most often been studied in terms of cultural differences. Blinco (1992) found that Japanese elementary school children showed greater task persistence than their American counterparts. School type and gender were not factors in moderating task persistence. This left culture as the remaining variable.
>
> Heine et al. (2001) furthered this idea by testing older American and Japanese subjects on responses after success or failure on task persistence. Japanese subjects were once again found to persist longer (in post-failure conditions), and this was speculated to be because they were more likely to view themselves as the cause of the problem. If they were the cause of the problem, they could also solve the problem themselves; although this could only be accomplished through work and persistence. Americans were more likely to believe that outside factors were the cause of failure.
>
> These cultural studies hinted that task persistence may be predictable based on attribution style. A later experiment showed that attribution style and perfectionism level can be correlated with final grades in college-level classes (Blankstein & Winkworth, 2004).

（文献来源：Adrian Wallwork, *English for Writing Research Papers*, New York: Springer, 2016, pp. 268-269.）

Analysis

The first sentence of the first paragraph introduces the main topic (cultural differences), and the rest of the paragraph briefly reviews a major study on this topic. The implications of this study (culture as the remaining variable) are summarized at the end of the paragraph.

The first sentence of the second paragraph then moves on to the next (in chronological terms) major study. Chris summarizes Heine's work in a way that involves the reader: he uses the verb speculated and then continues the next sentence using if which gives an example of this speculation.

文献综述和书评 | Literature Review and Book Review

The first sentence of the third paragraph summarizes the findings of the first two paragraphs in order to introduce some more recent findings.

Note also his use of tenses. In his first sentence, which is a very general overview, he uses the present perfect. Then when he talks about the work of specific authors and makes a summary of each step in the chronology of the literature he uses the past simple.

Chris's structure is thus:

1. introduction to topic
2. support from the literature
3. mini summary
4. introduction to next topic. And so on.

This technique works very well because it tells a story—it is a logical build up to the reason behind Chris's investigation that readers can easily follow. In fact, the final sentence to his Introduction begins: Because of these findings, I hypothesize that... Chris has gradually prepared his readers for the focus of his work: his own personal hypothesis regarding persistence.

Supplementary Readings 拓展阅读

CONTENT AND PROCESS THEORIES

The various theories of motivation are usually divided into content theories and process theories. The former attempt to "develop an understanding of fundamental human needs" (Cooper et al., 1992: 20). Among the most significant are Maslow's hierarchy of needs theory, McClellan's achievement theory and Herzberg's two-factor theory. The process theories deal with the actual methods of motivating workers, and include the work of Vroom, Locke and Adams.

Content Theories

Maslow's hierarchy of needs theory was first published in 1943 and envisages a pyramid of needs on five levels, each of which has to be satisfied before moving up to the next level. The first level is physiological needs such as food and drink, followed by security, love, esteem and self-fulfilment (Rollinson,

2005: 195–196). This theory was later revised by Alderfer, who reduced the needs to three: existence, relatedness and growth, and re-named it the ERG theory. In addition, he suggested that all three needs should be addressed simultaneously (Steers et al., 2004: 381). McClelland had a slightly different emphasis when he argued that individuals were primarily motivated by three principal needs: for achievement, affiliation and power (Mullins, 2006: 199).

In contrast, Herzberg suggested, on the basis of multiple interviews with engineers and accountants during the 1950s, a two-factor theory: that job satisfaction and dissatisfaction had differing roots. He claimed that so-called hygiene factors such as conditions and pay were likely to cause negative attitudes if inadequate, while positive attitudes came from the nature of the job itself. In other words, workers were satisfied if they found their work intrinsically interesting, but would not be motivated to work harder merely by good salaries or holiday allowances. Instead workers needed to be given more responsibility, more authority or more challenging tasks to perform (Vroom and Deci, 1992: 252). Herzberg's work has probably been the most influential of all the theories in this field, and is still widely used today, despite being the subject of some criticism, which will be considered later.

Process Theories

Vroom's expectancy theory hypothesizes a link between effort, performance and motivation. It is based on the idea that an employee believes that increased effort will result in improved performance. This requires a belief that the individual will be supported by the organization in terms of training and resources (Mullins, 2006). In contrast, Locke emphasized the importance of setting clear targets to improve worker performance in his goal theory. Setting challenging but realistic goals is necessary for increasing employee motivation: "goal specificity, goal difficulty and goal commitment each served to enhance task performance" (Steers et al., 2004: 382). This theory has implications for the design and conduct of staff appraisal systems and for management by objective methods focusing on the achievement of agreed performance targets.

Another approach was developed by Adams in his theory of equity, based on the concept that people value fairness. He argued that employees appreciate

文献综述和书评 | Literature Review and Book Review

> being treated in a transparently equitable manner in comparison with other workers doing similar functions, and respond positively if this is made apparent (Mullins, 2006). This approach takes a wider view of the workplace situation than some other theories, and stresses the balance each worker calculates between "inputs", i.e., the effort made, and "outputs", which are the rewards obtained.

（文献来源：Stephen Bailey, *Academic Writing: A Handbook for International Students*, New York: Routledge, 2015, pp. 212-213.）

Reading Comprehension

1. How many types of motivation theory are described?

2. How many different theorists are mentioned?

3. How many sources are cited?

4. Why has the writer not referred to the work of the theorists directly but used secondary sources instead?

Section 2 | Book Review 书评

Basic Knowledge 基础知识

Introduction

Book review gives a student the opportunity to critically examine a topic in detail. In general, a book review should contain two parts:

1. A description of the scope and organization of the book. Who is the author, and what has he or she written before? What kind of reader is the book aimed at? In the case of an edited volume, who are the editors and principal contributors?

2. The second part should evaluate how successful the book is in its aims. It is better to avoid excessive praise or criticism, and to mention both positive and

negative features. Is the book breaking new ground and adding significantly to current debates? It is also worth commenting on the author's style, and how easy it is to read for specialist or non-specialist readers.

Writers are recommended to first read a selection of reviews in their subject area before attempting their own.

简介

学生写书评意味着有机会批判性地审视一本书的细节。大体上，一部书评包含两部分内容：

1. 对该书范围和结构的描述。作者是谁？他/她以前有过哪些作品？该书的读者是谁？如果是编著、主编和撰写者是谁？

2. 该书在多大程度上达到了其撰写的目的。最好避免过分的赞美和批评，要从优点和缺陷两方面分析。该书是否另辟蹊径，对当下的热点有明显贡献？同时也有必要评论作者的写作风格以及对于专业人士和非专业人士的阅读难度。

写书评之前最好提前阅读相关领域的系列评论。

Writing Requirement

To best write a book review, it is essential to keep track of the answers to the following questions, either as you read the book or as soon as you have finished it. All of the answers can then be incorporated into your review.

Sample Book Review Template

SUMMARY

Narration

● Who narrated the story?
● Was it first-person narration or third-person narration?
● Was the narrator a reliable source of information?

Setting

● Note the time period and location the book is set in.
● How did setting drive or influence the plot of the book?

Theme

● Note the overall theme or message of the book.

Genre

● What genre of literature was it?

● How did it compare to another work in this genre?

Author

● Name the author.

● Discuss any previous works.

● How did previous works compare with this work?

Plot

● Give a brief plot summary without giving away any key details.

EVALUATION

Your Opinion

● This is the most important part of the review.

● Did you like it? Why?

● Would you read more by this author? Why or why not?

● Would you encourage others to read this book? Why or why not?[①]

写作要求

　　一篇成功的书评离不开对以下问题的回答。这些答案即是构成书评的重要部分。

书评结构模板

摘要

叙述

● 谁讲述了这个故事?

● 讲述的视角是第一人称还是第三人称?

● 讲述者的信息是否可靠?

背景设定

● 该书的时间和地点背景是什么?

● 背景设定如何影响了情节发展?

---

① http://www. wikihow. com/Sample/Book-Review-Template

主题
● 该书的主题或主要传达的信息是什么?
类型
● 该书属于哪种文献类型?
● 该书和同类型的文献有何异同点?
作者
● 作者的名字
● 作者以前的作品
● 该书和作者以前作品的比较
情节
● 简单概述该书的主要情节
评论
你的观点
● 这是书评最重要的部分
● 你喜欢吗? 为什么?
● 你愿意阅读该作者更多的作品吗? 为什么?
● 你愿意把书推荐给其他人吗? 为什么?

Case Studies 案例分析

Behind Closed Doors	
Ngaire Thomas, privately published, 2 Alaska Court, Palmerston North, New Zealand, www.behind-closed-doors.org, 2004. 294pp. ISBN 0646499106. NZ$34.	Bibliographic information
Behind Closed Doors is an inside look at what goes on behind the doors of the Exclusive Brethren. The book answers the question of what it is like to be a member of a select group who believe they are chosen to maintain the only pure path of Christianity. The author, Ngaire Thomas, was born into the church in the 1940s and left in the 1970s.	Introduction Statement of book's purpose Statement about the author

文献综述和书评 | Literature Review and Book Review

It is probably just coincidence that this book was launched at roughly the same time that sociologist Bryan Wilson died. Wilson published the definitive	Places the book in a context
study on the Exclusive Brethren in 1967, and was an expert witness in their court cases. Wilson's conclusions were based on information the religion provided about itself; he dismissed ex-members' accounts as suspect atrocity stories and warned courts not to give credence to their testimony. i Today, after outbreaks of violence in other religions have repeatedly demonstrated that ex-members accounts are often more accurate than academic ones,ii we may be more welcoming of their insights.	Statement about book's genre and potential significance
As one such ex-member account, Ngaire Thomas' book is compelling. Her style is non-judgemental; she describes her experiences while acknowledging the Exclusive Brethren's right to follow a religious path in which they find meaning.	Overall evaluation
The book begins with Ngaire's childhood. She is different from the other children with her long dresses and strict upbringing. She loves school because it is the only place that she can be her real self. Worldly things are forbidden: there are no radios (because Satan rules the airwaves) or non-Brethren books. Life revolves around the *Bible*, and when Ngaire brings friends home from school her mother preaches to them about the end times in Revelation. Other Christians are also deemed suspect, and Ngaire recalls getting the strap when caught secretly attending *Bible* in School classes.	Summary of the book's beginning — giving details which provide the context of the author's conflict

（文献来源：http://owll. massey. ac. nz/assignment-types/book-review. php）

33

Supplementary Readings
拓展阅读

> This useful and important edited volume partly fills a gap in the comparative political science literature. The book compares the society and politics of the European Union (treated here as a single state) with the United States. The book examines "convergences and divergences" between these two global powers, similar in size and economic weight "but asymmetric in terms of political influence and military might" (p.1).
>
> The book has eight chapters. The introductory and concluding chapters, which hold the volume together, are written by the editor. The first briefly outlines the adopted comparative approach and methodological challenges faced in producing this study. Montero then goes on to argue that the EU and the US offer two contrasting models of Western modernity. The final chapter argues that the process of constructing the EU has led to convergence, not divergence, between the EU and the US. In between are six sectoral chapters; of particular interest is the third, by Kuhl, which argues that the quality of the democratic experience is in decline on both sides of the Atlantic.
>
> This is a well-written work that breaks new ground in treating the EU as a single state. However, the book was published in 2008, a year after the EU had enlarged to 27 states. The authors fail to deal fully with this "geographic boundary" problem. This neglect of the newest member states is repeated throughout the volume and brings into question the validity of the book's wider conclusions.

（文献来源：Marcus Montero, *Atlantic Crossing: A Comparison of European and American Society*, York: York University Press, 2008, p. 378.）

Reading Comprehension

Study the above review and discuss with a partner whether there is anything else that you think the reviewer should have included.

文献综述和书评 | Literature Review and Book Review

Exercise 课后练习

● **True or False**

Directions: Read the following sentences and decide whether they are true or false.

1. In most papers a literature review is included in the conclusion.
2. Book reviews may be written by graduate students for academic journals in order to broaden their knowledge and achieve publication.
3. It is allowed to provide a shopping list of past papers in writing a literature review.

● **Gap-Filling**

Directions: Complete each sentence with appropriate words.

1. Occasionally, the whole focus of an essay may be a lengthy literature review, but in most student writing it will only form a relatively short section of the paper. Only a minority have a separate section headed "_____" or "_____".
2. To best write a book review, it is essential to keep track of the _____ to the important questions, either as you read the book or as soon as you have finished it. All of the answers can then be incorporated into your own _____.

● **Short Answer Questions**

Directions: Answer the following questions briefly.

1. What is the key to the literature review?
2. Generally, what are the two parts that should be included in a book review?

● **Simulative Exercise**

Based on your understanding of the purpose and methods of book review writing, choose one of the most impressive academic books you have read and write a book review about it.

Application Essay
申请书

Abstract
内容概览

This chapter provides assistance to those who are about to apply to colleges that require an essay as part of the application process. Some authors are, at most, intimidated, or, at least, uncomfortable with such a task. They may attempt to overcome individual fears by restoring confidence and causing natural abilities to surface.

Colleges require the essay because it is the easiest way to find out what you are made of. They like the way in which it offers applicants the opportunity to reveal their persona, to exercise their imagination, to draw upon their experience, to parade their grammatical skills, to use an appropriate vocabulary, and to make whatever point they wish.

在申请学校的过程中,同学们需要写一篇文章,本章的内容就是为此类同学提供帮助的。同学们或多或少都会对此类任务感到不适,甚至害怕。其实可以通过恢复信心和提升自身能力来克服个人恐惧。

撰写文章是使得学校了解你个人能力的最简单办法。他们青睐这种方法是因为这可为学生提供机会来展示个性、锻炼想象力、总结自身经验、展现语法技巧、使用恰当词汇以及表达个人的任何观点。

申请书 | Application Essay

Basic Knowledge
基础知识

Introduction

Success at any school depends on knowing what you're in for; nothing is more bitter than disappointed expectations. The essay is particularly useful in determining the fit between the applicant and the college. David Wagner at Hampshire, says, "Our students design their own programs through negotiation with faculty advisers. We need to be sure they have the motivation and vision to do that. The essay is one of the places we look for confirmation." If a college has a particular character — its curriculum is tightly focused (Fashion Institute of Technology, the U. S. service academies) or it relies on a special teaching methodology (Sarah Lawrence College) or curriculum (St. John's great books program), the essay can reflect an understanding of and enthusiasm for this special setting.

Clearly, the essay adds to the overall pattern of your application. The colleges take it seriously; you should too. It is part of your need to compete and the college's need to select. "The essay can be a powerful 'tipper' in close cases, especially with very strong or very poor essays," says Bates' Bill Hiss. If an essay is required or even allowed, use it to present yourself effectively. Remember, it is a separate part of the application and should convey information not found elsewhere. If you ignore this advice, you defeat the college's purpose in requesting an essay. Seize this opportunity to stand out from the similar recommendations, and the other kids.

Remember, the essay should not be an explanation of grades or exceptional circumstances in your background. If your grades and scores are not reflective of your ability, the essay is, of course, another chance to shine.[①]

简介

能否成功申请一所学校的关键在于你是否清楚自己在做什么；没有什么是比在失望中还抱有期待更令人痛苦的了。申请书在确定申请人与所申请学校的要求是否契合这方面格外有用。来自汉普郡学院的大卫·瓦格纳说："我们的

---

① Sarah M. McGinty, *The College Application Essay*, New York: College Board, 2015.

学生通过与教师顾问的沟通来设计自己的课程。我们需要确保他们有这样的动机和远见。这份申请书即是我们寻求确认的要点之一。"如果一个学院有自身的特性——它的课程紧密集中（如美国军事院校的时装技术学院）或依赖一种特殊的教学方法（萨拉劳伦斯学院）或课程（圣约翰好书计划），这份申请书可以很好地反映出申请人对这些偏好的理解与热爱。

显而易见的是，这篇文章可以提升申请书的总体格局。这正是学校所看重的一点，作为学生也应该如此。这是你用来与别人竞争的一部分，同时也是学校用来筛选学生的一部分。来自贝茨学院的比尔·希斯教授说："在条件相近的情况下，此申请书可以作为一个非常有力的证明材料，尤其是对于那些非常优秀和非常差劲的文章来说。"如果（申请的学校）允许甚至是需要（你所撰写的）一篇文章，你应该有效地利用它来展示自己。请记住，这是你申请材料中的一个独立部分，应当在其中传达出别处没有的信息。倘若你忽视了该建议，你将会与学校的要求和用意背道而驰。抓住这个机会，你将会在与相似的推荐信的遴选中，以及与他人的竞争中等方面脱颖而出。

请记住，此篇文章不应是对你个人背景中的成绩或者特殊情况的解释。如果你的成绩并不能较好地反映你个人的能力，这篇文章自然将会是你另一个脱颖而出的机会。

Writing Requirement

The number one piece of advice from admission officers about your essay is "Be yourself". The number two suggestion is "Start early". Check out these other tips before you begin.

Choose a Topic That Will Highlight You

Don't focus on the great aspects of a particular college, the amount of dedication it takes to be a doctor or the number of extracurricular activities you took part in during high school.

Do share your personal story and thoughts, take a creative approach and highlight areas that aren't covered in other parts of the application, like your high school records.

Top two tips: Be yourself and start early

Keep Your Focus Narrow and Personal

Don't try to cover too many topics. This will make the essay sound like a résumé that doesn't provide any details about you.

申请书 | Application Essay

Do focus on one aspect of yourself so the readers can learn more about who you are. Remember that the readers must be able to find your main idea and follow it from beginning to end. Ask a parent or teacher to read just your introduction and tell you what he or she thinks your essay is about.

Show, Don't Tell

Don't simply state a fact to get an idea across, such as "I like to surround myself with people with a variety of backgrounds and interests".

Do include specific details, examples, reasons and so on to develop your ideas. For the example above, describe a situation when you were surrounded by various types of people. What were you doing? Whom did you talk with? What did you take away from the experience?

Use Your Own Voice

Don't rely on phrases or ideas that people have used many times before. These could include statements like, "There is so much suffering in the world that I feel I have to help people". Avoid overly formal or business-like language, and don't use unnecessary words.

Do write in your own voice. For the above example, you could write about a real experience that you had and how it made you feel you had to take action. And note that admission officers will be able to tell if your essay was edited by an adult.

Ask a Teacher or Parent to Proofread

Don't turn your essay in without proofreading it, and don't rely only on your computer's spell check to catch mistakes. A spell-check program will miss typos like these:

"After I graduate from high school, I plan to get a summer job."

"From that day on, Daniel was my best friend."

Do ask a teacher or parent to proofread your essay to catch mistakes. You should also ask the person who proofreads your essay if the writing sounds like you.[①]

写作要求

关于你的文章，招生官给的第一条建议就是："做你自己"。第二个建议

---

① Sarah M. McGinty, *The College Application Essay*, New York: College Board, 2015.

则是"尽早开始"。在开始你的写作之前，请阅读以下建议。

选择一个能突出你个人的话题。

不要把焦点集中于某一所大学的各个方面，比如成为一名医生所需要的奉献精神，或是你在高中时参加的课外活动的数量。

分享你的个人故事与想法，采取一种创造性的方法来突出申请书其他部分没有覆盖的领域，比如你的高中履历。

最关键的两点建议：做你自己，尽早开始。

缩小关注领域，重点关注自身。

不要试着去涵盖太多话题。这会使得你的文章看起来像简历，且无法提供关于你自身的任何细节。

一定要专注于自己的某一个方面，这样读者就能更多地了解你自己。记住，读者必须能够找到你的主要观点，并愿意从头读到尾。请父母或老师阅读你的简介，并告诉你在他/她看来，你文章的主题是什么。

描述，而不是陈述。

不要简单地陈述或者是得出一个想法，比如"我喜欢让自己周围有各种各样的背景和兴趣的人"。

一定要包括具体的细节、例子、理由等等来充实你的想法。在上面的例子中，请描述出当你被各种各样的人包围的时候，你在做什么？你和谁有过交流？你从此次经历中得到了什么？

使用你自己的语言方式。

不要依赖陈词滥调。如："世界上有太多的痛苦，我觉得我必须帮助别人"等此类说明方式。避免过于正式或商业化的语言，不要使用不必要的词语。

一定要用你自己的语言方式来写。在上面的例子中，你可以写下你的真实经历，以及它如何让你觉得你必须采取行动。请注意，如果你的文章是由一个成年人代笔的，招生官会很轻易看出来。

请老师或家长来校对。

不要在没有校对的情况下提交你的文章，不要只依赖电脑的拼写检查来发现错误。拼写检查程序会漏掉以下此类的错误，如：

"After I graduate from high school, I plan to get a summer job."

"From that day on, Daniel was my best friend."

请老师或家长校对你的文章，以找出错误。此外，你应该询问校对者，此文的行文风格是否听起来像是你本人写的。

申请书 | Application Essay

Case Studies
案例分析

　　The alarm clock is, To many high school students, a wailing monstrosity whose purpose is to torture all who are sleep-deprived.

　　Those who believe this are misguided, and are simply viewing the situation from a twisted perspective. For when these imprudent early-risers blearily rub their eyes each morning, and search in vain for whatever is making that earsplitting noise, they are, without a doubt, annoyed.

　　Why?

　　It isn't because the only thing they desire is to sleep a few extra hours, as many would presume. No, these kids are groggy and irritable because they are waking up to what they think will be another horribly boring day of school. If one of these foolish Sallys or Joes were, say, sleeping comfortably on a Saturday morning, I could certainly see something different happening. A beautiful breakfast of tantalizing vittles—eggs, hash browns, and the like—would be ready and waiting for them on their kitchen tables. But the scrumptious delight to outshine them all would be a slab of bacon, piled proudly for the taking. It would be that wafting, wondrous bacon smell that would draw dear, sweet Sally abruptly from her slumber—long before an alarm clock has the chance to pierce the air.

　　Oh, bacon: what a marvelous, glorious thing! I live for those heart stoppingly good strips of succulence, so crispy and crunchy, so packed with perfection. The thought of having a plate of bacon every day, perhaps every school day, sends me into sheer waves of ecstasy!

　　To be sure, many others would also wax poetic about this lovely breakfast food. But precious few would share this same zeal for learning. I, however, can smugly decree that I do regard both very highly. I brightly waken every morning to the mellifluous joy that sounds from my alarm clock, a huge smile plastered on my face, and the yearning to learn in my heart.

　　When I board my school bus Monday through Friday, it is still pitch black outside. Bus mates will groan about how even the day has not yet dragged itself out of bed; I only chuckle through their thirty-minute rant fest as we chug down the freeway. Opting to be part of a faraway Magnet school, after all, has its benefits. My peers may still not look forward to waking up earlier, but when we are all together in a classroom, we take on the "bacon mentality". I have the opportunity to choose from a wealth of diverse classes, and love arriving to school each day with the prospect of having a new Spanish History lesson—taught to me in Spanish, for a change. Teachers, driven by the enthusiasm of their Magnet students, are inspired to create new classes for advanced students, including those who have completed AP Spanish Literature and are still eager to learn more, or those who want to learn about a specific aspect of a subject—we now have a Middle Eastern History class. Not to be outdone, the post-AP exam period of my English Language class included an intensive literature study, where we laughed at good ol' Yossarian in Catch-22, and developed a strong attachment to Jay Gatsby. I'd like to think that The Great Gatsby's pursuit of Daisy is not unlike my own pursuit of bacon. I've gobbled up new knowledge rapidly, hankering after it like any elusive bacon strip, and happily digesting any new bits of information.

But six classes a year are simply not enough to satisfy my hunger for knowledge. Just as I eat bacon all three meals of the day (when possible), I attempt to learn all days of the week. Rather than make another trip to some lackluster movie theatre on the weekend, I dedicate my time to reading another good book, or reviewing Economics with my friends. But high school is starting to smell like leftovers to me now; I want fresh, new, crisp learning. I want not to read a textbook written by a renowned professor: I want to hear him speak directly. I'm ready for the university, and hunger for all the new opportunities waiting for me!

I've finished my breakfast, and now it's time to get going to school.

（文献来源：Gen Tanabe, and Kelly Tanabe. *50 Successful Ivy League Application Essays.* Super College, 2015, pp. 21-23. ）

Analysis

Mariam's essay "Bacon" uses lively language and plenty of humor to tell a story that highlights her eagerness to go to school. Her writing is casual and funny, and it conveys in a personal and genuine way her enthusiastic attitude. "Bacon" reminds us that topics do not have to be serious to be sincere.

The metaphor of bacon is a very memorable one in image, smell, texture, and taste. Mariam capitalizes on these features in her beautiful—and mouthwatering!—descriptors of a Saturday morning breakfast of eggs. With a touch of humor and a hint of parody, she writes, "Oh, bacon: what a marvelous, glorious thing! I live for those heart stoppingly good strips of succulence, so crispy and crunchy, so packed with perfection. The thought of having a plate of bacon every day, perhaps every school day, sends me into sheer waves of ecstasy!"

Just when this celebration of bacon begins to appear over-the-top, and readers are beginning to worry that Mariam swapped a food magazine piece with her college admissions essay, she links the succulent bacon metaphor with school: "To be sure, many others would also wax poetic about this lovely breakfast food. But precious few would share this same zeal for learning." Though Mariam takes a risk in waxing poetic over bacon, she does so with carefully calculated dramatic effect that ultimately pays off. We are convinced that the "yearning to learn" is deeply engrained in our bacon-lover and early-riser author.

Mariam's narrative also shows us the sacrifices she makes for attending a Magnet school far from home. Her use of the phrase "bacon mentality" is original and creative. Mariam's descriptions of her classes are specific enough to prevent them from reading like a list. Rather, she demonstrates the depth of her commitment in her classes by citing specific details like Yossarian in Catch-22. Mariam's essay demonstrates how she is able to ft impressive details of her life into a narrative framework, a strategy that can avoid the pitfall of sounding like bragging. Mariam follows the "show, don't tell" mantra when she mentions the Magnet school in the context of her long early-morning bus ride, and in celebrating her Spanish history class, which is impressively taught in Spanish.

At the end of the essay, the bacon metaphor may seem overdone to some readers, as Mariam has "gobbled up new knowledge rapidly, hankering after it like any elusive bacon strip" and has expressed a desire for "fresh, new crisp" learning to satisfy her "hunger for knowledge". She might have reduced the number of mentions of bacon and hunger. However, Mariam's essay ultimately stands out for its originality and unpredictable connections, like linking The Great Gatsby to—what else?—bacon.

Supplementary Readings
拓展阅读

  I finally have been taken out of the intensive care in the hospital and my name has been removed from the critical list, but I am still awaiting a complete recovery from a disease that all American Chinese have and that a few, like I, dread. This disease lies dormant in most American Chinese, but becomes malignant in the other unfortunate few. The symptoms of this disease are bipartitely divided, the first group of symptoms belonging to the majority of Chinese not malignantly affected by this disease. Their symptoms bring contentment, joy, and the assurance of a bright future. The second group belongs to those who are malignantly affected. Their symptoms bring anxiety, frustration, and deep pain. What is this bizarre malady that can bring either so much happiness or so much anguish? It is the Chinese Syndrome, a disease that only afflicts families with children.

  It is not too hard to recognize the majority. They are the ABC's (American Born Chinese) with the 4.0 grade point averages and enough medals from piano competitions to recast the Statue of Liberty in gold. They are the ones who destroy all hopes of receiving a much needed curve on the AP Calculus II test. The minority is also quite easy to recognize. They are the ones who like seeing how many words they can assemble from their grades. They, however, often find themselves unable to form a coherent word because they lack a vowel. The majority also have a problem forming words. No matter how hard they try, they always end up sounding like Fonz on "Happy Days".

  Where do the roots of this horrible disease lie? They lie, of course, within the parents. All parents, whether they are from the majority or the minority, have one tragic flaw: they are constantly in search of the elusive commodity called pride. It is a pride that lies in the parent's child who graduated from AP High as valedictorian or, with some reluctance of the parents, salutatorian. Many parents, in fact, perverse the function of dinner parties by creating family feuds

申请书 | Application Essay

in the living room of the hostess. Parents launch ICBMs (Incredibly Bombastic Material) of what stupendous grades and awards their children have recently acquired. Other families retaliate with barrages of how late their son stays up at night doing his homework or practicing piano. Even the hostess takes a good swing to the guests by blinding them with her daughter's violin competition awards as they walk through the door. But, what happens to the minorities' parents? They quietly slump down in their chairs, wishing that they were some miniscule blob in the next room.

These parents, however, get their revenge for this shocking embarrassment by dashing home and taking the culprit who must have mistakenly been born as their child and assailing him with the dreaded "look-at-Doug-who-got-a-690-verbal-and-a-780-math-and-won-the-state-competition-in-piano-and-gotinto-Harvard" lecture. Even as the shell-shocked child limps away, he can still hear his parents ranting and raving in the kitchen below, asking why did they not get a child like Doug?

The strain and stress of these battered children is enormous. They cannot help but feel pain, frustration, and uselessness when they see that their achievements do not matchup to their friends. I was once one of those orphans left out in the cold until I found the only possible cure for this disease. I found myself.

I finally was able to see my own special talents that define who I really am. With this discovery, I also found myself worth and the ability to believe in myself. I no longer mope about the house, wondering why I was not blessed with the ability that many other Chinese have. Now, I realize that the talents I do have are special and unique in me.

Through my experience with this disease, a sense of maturity and self-realization has evolved. I am grateful for the efforts of my parents who are trying valiantly to prepare me for the future by making me the best that I can ever be. Often, we, the minority, feel that our parents' attitude toward the whole matter of being Chinese belongs in another century and world, but we must recognize our parents' concern for our future. Frequently, we are too shortsighted to see this. It is true that our parents are looking for pride, but everyone needs something to be proud about and there is nothing better than a parent being proud of his or her child.

Alas, this disease, the Chinese Syndrome, will never fade away. It will always be there to torment those few unfortunate Chinese who have not yet found themselves. Until they do so, they are lost in a world of sermons that last late into the night.

We often find ourselves saying like Othello: "Farewell tranquil mind, farewell content." I still find myself studying hard in order to stay up with the pack that we Chinese make up.

Within that pack is a gamut of raw talent and energy. It does not matter that I may not be like the majority of Chinese children. I am proud to be Chinese.

（文献来源：Kenneth A. Nourse, *How to Write College Application Essay,* New York: McGraw-Hill Companies, 2001, pp. 29-30）

Reading Comprehension

1. What are features of this application?
2. What makes this application different from the one in case study?
3. Is there any place in this application that needs to be improved?

Exercise
课后练习

● **True or False**

Directions: Read the following sentences and decide whether they are true or false.

1. Do try to cover many topics to develop your ideas.
2. Keep your focus wide and personal.
3. Don't hand in your essay without proofreading.

申请书 | Application Essay

● Gap-Filling

Directions: Complete each sentence with appropriate words.

1. Do share your _____ and thoughts, take a creative approach and _____ areas that aren't covered in other parts of the application, like your high school records.
2. Do include specific _____, _____, _____ and so on to develop your ideas.
3. Don't turn your essay in without _____ it, and don't rely only on your computer's spell check to catch mistakes.

● Short Answer Questions

Directions: Answer the following questions briefly.

1. What is the advice provided by admission officer?
2. Can you cover too many topics in your essay? Why?

● Simulative Exercise

Try to write down one of your own stories or experiences, and use specific details, examples, reasons and so on to develop it.

Chapter 5

Resume and CV
简历和履历

Abstract
内容概览

Finding a great job starts with writing a great resume/CV, one that speaks to your personal and professional strengths. Learn how to write a resume/CV that stands out and makes employers take notice.

Resumes and CVs are tools used to introduce job seekers to potential employers. A resume is a relatively short listing of a candidate's qualifications, employment history and achievements. Resume basics tend to dictate that this marketing tool favor brevity, although resume styles can vary. CVs, on the other hands, call for more details about a candidate. CV styles can also vary, but most include work history, achievements and skills of a candidate. Improving your resume or CV can be an important step toward landing a position. It is helpful to review sample resumes and CVs to get ideas for appearance, content and formatting.

找一份好工作都是以一份好简历或者履历开始的，简历和履历是用来证明你的个人能力和专业优势的材料。学习如何写好一份简历或履历会使你在所有求职者中脱颖而出，让雇主注意到你。

简历和履历是用来给潜在雇主介绍求职者的工具。简历是一份相对简短的关于应聘者的任职资格、工作经历和成就的清单列表。简历的基本特征在于其简洁性，但是它的样式风格可以变化。而履历对应聘者来说要求更多的细节。履历的样式也可变化，但是大部分内容涉及应聘者的工作经历、成就和技能。改善你的简历或履历是获得一个职位的重要一步。反复揣摩简历和履历的范本有助于改进样式、内容和格式，这对求职者来说有很大的帮助。

Section 1 | Resume 简历

Basic Knowledge 基础知识

Introduction

The word "resume" comes from the French for "to summarize," which is the purpose of a resume: to summarize your education and experience for your potential employer in a way that positions you as a good candidate for the job.

Prospective employers may receive hundreds of resumes for any one job, and their time is limited. Therefore, you want to make sure that your resume will help you stand out among all the other applicants as a good fit for the position by tailoring the information you include to your audience and to the position description. Your integrity is important, so make sure that anything you include on your resume is accurate and will stand up to questioning in an interview.

简介

"简历"这个单词来源于法语，本意为"概况、总结"，这也是简历的目的所在：总结概括你的教育学历和社会经历。从某种程度上来说，它是你的潜在雇主聘用你成为这份工作的候选人的标准之一。

未来的雇主会因为任何一份工作而收到成百上千份简历，但是他们的时间是有限的，因此想要让你的简历在所有求职者中脱颖而出，就必须根据你的面试官和职位描述适当调整你的信息来适应这份工作。你的诚信至关重要，因此请确保您简历中包含的任何内容都准确无误，以经得起面试提问环节的考验。

Writing Requirement

Your resume should be divided into clearly labeled sections that allow your prospective employer to skim through and learn about your relevant experience. The tables below explain the required and possible sections you can have in your resume. These are just some of the possible sections. There may be others specific to your field, or others that reflect your strengths and that are relevant for a particular job, so make sure to get advice from advisers, faculty and professionals about what sections to include.①

Section Name	Details
Contact Information	This section should be at the top of your page and include your name, your phone number, your address, and your email.
Education	Starting with college, include which school you are attending, your major, your degree type, and your expected degree year. Only include your GPA if it will impress your employer (above a 3.4 on a four-point scale is a good rule of thumb).
Work Experience	This is the heart of your resume. Include your job title, your employer, the time span you worked, and the location where you worked. Use your active verbs and keywords to describe work experience in bullet points with two to three bullets under each job. Use present tense verbs for current jobs and past tense verbs for past jobs.
Honors and Awards	An honors and awards section highlights that you have been recognized as exceptional in an area relevant to your job. The section should include the name of the award and the year received.

写作要求

你的简历应该包括栏目分明的几部分，这样方便你未来的雇主快速浏览并了解你的相关经历。下面这张表格解释了你在简历中需要和可能用到的部分。这里介绍的仅仅是一些可能用到的部分，还有其他部分，比如针对你的具体领域，或者能反映出你的优势，与你特定工作相关的部分。因此要努力从就业顾问、教师和专家那里获得简历应该包含哪些部分的建议。

---

① Resume Writing Tips: The least you need to know about writing a resume. https://writing.wisc.edu/Handbook/Resume.html

简历和履历 | Resume and CV

内容名称	具体介绍
基本信息和联系方式	这一部分应该在你简历的顶部，包括姓名、电话号码、家庭住址和电子邮箱。
学历	先写大学，包括就读学校、专业、学位等级和预期学位年。最好写上你的平均绩点，如果它能给你的雇主留下深刻印象（四分制中平均绩点在3.4以上的可以写在学历中）。
工作经历	这一部分是你简历的核心，包括你的工作岗位、雇主、工作时间、工作地点。用主动语态和关键词来描述你的工作经历，并加上项目符号，每个工作下面有两到三个项目符号就够了。使用现在时态表示现在的工作，过去时态表示过去的工作。
荣誉和奖励	荣誉和奖励的部分要强调与你工作相关的领域内获得的荣誉，这会使雇主认为你很杰出、优秀。这部分应该包括你的获奖名称和获奖的年份。

Case Studies 案例分析

	Your Name	
1705 Monroe Street Madison, WI 53711	firstnamelastname@wisc.edu	500 Silent Street Verona, WI 53593
Objective	Internship in nuclear engineering, particularly in fuels or reactor engineering.	
Education	University of Wisconsin-Madison B. S. /M. S. Nuclear Engineering and Engineering Physics, expected May 2013 • GPA: 3. 92/4. 0 • Distinguished Scholar • Certificate in Technical Japanese	

（续表）

Education	Academic Projects: Ionizing Radiation—Validation of DANTSYS computer model dose rates of UW Nuclear Reactor thermal column Independent Study—Flux measurements of the UW Nuclear Reactor following a core shuffle Coursework: Nuclear Reactor Theory; Nuclear Reactor Analysis, Nuclear Reactor Engineering, Radiation Damage in Metals; Multiphase Flow, Nuclear Reactor Design
Experience	University of Wisconsin Nuclear Reactor Laboratory, Madison, WI Reactor Operator, May 2010—Present • Operated the reactor on a regular basis to provide support for lasses, experiments, and training • Led tours of the reactor and surrounding lab for visitors with a variety of educational backgrounds • Encouraged and followed safe practices, such as ALARA, while working with radioactive materials and in radiation areas UTi Integrated Logistics, Racine, WI Special Handling, Summer 2009 • Promoted awareness and adherence to proper safety regulations and procedures when handling hazardous chemicals and products • Coordinated with a range of coworkers to consistently meet customer deadlines
Computer Skills	SolidWorks, Quantum Gold, AutoCAD, Matlab, Maple, MS Office, Engineering Equation Solver (EES); MCNP, Helios
Languages	Japanese (Technical), Conversational

（续表）

Academic Honors and Awards	Max W. Carbon Scholarship in Nuclear Technology, 2011-12
	Exelon Scholarship, 2010
	Nuclear Regulatory Commission Scholarship, 2009
	Tau Beta Pi Honor Society
	Dean's Honor List (6/6 Semesters)
Activities	American Nuclear Society
	National Society of Collegiate Scholars

References available upon request.

（文献来源：Resume Writing Tips, the Writing Center, University of Wisconsin-Madison, https://writing. wisc. edu/Handbook/SampleResume3. pdf. ）

Analysis

This resume is a complete one since it includes various parts, like objective, education, experience, computer skills, languages, academic honors and awards, etc. Meanwhile, it is noteworthy that various parts in the resume are not dealt with equally, as we can see that compared to other parts, both education and experience are more emphasized, which means these two parts carry more weight than others.

Supplementary Readings
拓展阅读

Read the resume and answer the following questions.

John A. Doe

    4120 Chevy Trail

    Ann Arbor, Michigan 48111-9626

    (111) 555-111

    johndoe@abc. com

SUMMARY

Experienced and versatile professional with strong systems planning, people, and research skills, with the ability to:

Direct transportation planning & programs

Manage programs and people

Anticipate & project for organizational change

Design & develop cost-saving systems

Administer office operations

EXPERIENCED IN THE FOLLOWING AREAS

Government guidelines ~ Environmental impact mitigation research

Urban planning ~ Geology/hydrology ~ Site evaluations

Computer software tools ~ Scientific/business/grant writing ~ Quality control

SKILLS

Administrative — Lead coordinator for the daily processing of thousands of checks for payment and the mailing of confidential reports, meeting strict deadlines, and avoiding late fees.

Problem Solving — Designed a waste management program involving Recycle Ann Arbor and a major book company, intended for the efficient handling of tons of paper, cardboard, plastic, metal, and glass, achieving net savings of $20,000 per building annually and reducing company disposal obligations.

Management — Oversaw operations of an expanding research lab, providing expertise, commitment, and quality control during a time of significant transition.

Organizational — Consolidated community awareness information into an effective and easy-to-use pocket guide for Bicycling in Ann Arbor, distributing them throughout the area to promote bicycle safety and ridership.

Cost Awareness — Verified the accuracy of office processes and expenses, eliminating overbilling and cultivating an attitude of quality control among staff.

Creative — Make transportation program literature, maps, and correspondences to politicians and agencies, employing innate abilities and formal training, resulting in program recognition and 20% increase in product use.

EXPERIENCE

Shepherd's Watch

Design and Research Consultant: Design, lay out, and assist in marketing sundials and assorted wearable and garden timepieces for a specialty company.

ACWG

Association of Pedestrian and Bicycle Professionals Member: Collaborate with other alternative transportation people to better develop pedestrian and bicycle-friendly communities.

APBP

Washtenaw Biking and Walking Coalition Advocate: Advocate bicycle and pedestrian use, rights, and responsibilities.

WBWC

Ann Arbor Bicycle Coordinating Committee Member: Guide bicycle program, road projects, parking, and facilities to include and encourage bicycle and alternative transportation.

City of Ann Arbor

Research Assistant I: Managed a large and growing science lab, overseeing legal compliance, as well as database and administrative duties.

EDUCATION

EASTERN MICHIGAN UNIVERSITY, Ypsilanti, Michigan

Bachelor of Science, 19XX

Major: Biology-Ecosystem/Environmental

Business and Fine Arts Concentrations

（文献来源：Alison Doyle, Example of a Functional Resume, https://www.thebalance. com/functional-resume-example-2063203.）

Reading Comprehension

1. Compare this resume and the one in the section of Case studies, what are the similarities between the two?
2. What are the features of this one?
3. Is there anything that needs to be improved?

Section 2 | CV 履历

Basic Knowledge 基础知识

Introduction

The term "CV" is short for "curriculum vitae"—the Latin phrase for "the course of one's life". Your CV is a document that presents who you are as a scholar. CVs are used in academic spheres to organize your education, experiences, and accomplishments in a clear and predictable way that allows readers to skim and find information efficiently. When you apply for an academic position or opportunity, a CV is usually requested instead of a resume.

Hiring committees may receive hundreds of applications for any one job, and their time is limited. Therefore, you want to make sure that your CV is as clear and directed as possible. Your CV needs to be tailored to that position's specific expectations and structured and formatted so that all your material is clear, consistent, and skimmable. Your integrity is very important to uphold, so as with any other application document, make sure that anything you include on your CV is accurate and will stand up to questioning in an interview.

While CVs and resumes are similar documents, they are also different in some key ways. This table details some of the most important points of comparison and contrast to be aware of:[①]

---

① CV Writing Tips: An Introduction to Writing a CV. https://writing. wisc. edu/Handbook/CV. html

简历和履历 | Resume and CV

	Resume	CV
Purpose	To present the case that your experience and skills make you a great candidate for a particular position.	To present the case that your academic experience and accomplishments make you a great candidate for a particular academic position.
Audience	Any possible employer or HR employee.	Fellow academics on a hiring committee.
Length	Probably only 1 page and absolutely no longer than 2 pages.	As long as you need it to be while still keeping it as concise as possible.
Content Description of Experience	Focused on active skills linked with quantifiable results you've achieved.	Often not needed since your audience understands academic work and many job, publication, and conference titles are self-explanatory.
Objective Statement	May appear on the top of the first page.	Not included.
References	Not included.	May appear at the end of the CV.
Formatting	Simple, clear, and skimmable.	Simple, clear, and skimmable.

简介

CV 是"curriculum vitae"的缩写，它是拉丁语词组，意思是某人一生的概况。履历是展现你作为一名学者的文件。履历通常被用于学术范围内，以清楚和可预料的方式总结你的学历、经验和学术成就，使读者能高效地浏览并找出重要信息。当你申请大学或者研究所里的教职、研究职位时，履历往往比简历更适用。

招聘委员会每次会因为同一份职位而收到成百上千的申请书，但是他们筛选这些求职信的时间是有限的。因此，你要确保你的履历尽可能地简明扼要。你的履历需要根据该职位的特定要求量身定制，具有良好的结构组织和格式，这样就会使你的材料显得清晰、连贯、便于浏览。就像其他求职申请书一样，你的诚信非常重要，因此请确保您在履历中包含的任何内容都准确无误，并能在面试中接受质疑。

尽管履历和简历这两类文档相似，但是它们在一些关键方面还是有区别的。下面这张表详尽地说明了履历和简历在类比时应该注意的几点：

	简历	履历
目的	为了展现你的经历和技能，使你成为这份工作的优秀候选人。	为了展现你的学术经历和学术成就，使你成为这份学术职位的优秀候选人。
读者	任何潜在雇主和人力资源职员。	招聘委员会的学术界同行。
长度	可能只有一页，或者绝对不超过两页的篇幅。	尽可能使它简洁，篇幅没有简历限制严格，它根据你的需求所定。
内容/经验描述	侧重于成果可量化的各项技能。	一般不太需要，因为你的读者理解学术著作、学术工作、出版物和学术会议名称都是不需要加以说明的。
客观陈述	可能出现在第一页的顶端开头。	不需要。
参考	不需要。	可能出现在履历的末尾。
格式	简单，清楚，方便浏览的。	简单，清楚，方便浏览的。

Writing Requirement

Your CV should be divided into clearly labeled sections that allow your readers to easily skim through and learn about your relevant qualifications. The exact sections you include will depend on your background and the positions you're applying for. In some disciplines, there may be an established order to the sections after "Education". If so, follow that. If not, highlight your greatest strengths for the position. For example, if you are applying for a position at a research university, you might choose to start with your publications. If the position primarily involves teaching, lead with your teaching section. In what follows, we detail the most common CV sections:

Contact Information

This information should appear at the top of your CV and should include your name, phone number, mailing address (either work or private), and professional email address. You may want to draw some attention to this information by slightly altering the formatting, alignment, or font, but don't overdo this.

Education

Frequently this section follows your contact information. This section, like most in a CV, is organized in reverse chronological order, so that your most recent (or highest) degree or degree-in-progress appears first. Include the name of the school, the degree conferred, the area of study and/or major and minor, and the year the degree was completed. This is also an appropriate place to include the title of your dissertation and/or Master's thesis along with your key advisors' names. Don't include your GPA, and generally, do not include information about anything prior to your Bachelor's degree.

Employment Experience

Given the expectations of a CV, include only employment experience that is connected to your academic work, interests, and development. Also, whereas in a resume you describe your work, skills, and accomplishments, such detailed descriptions are often out of place in a CV. The people reading your CV have a pretty good idea of what it means to have taught, for example, a general chemistry or an introduction to philosophy course. Of course, if a position you held wouldn't be clear to other academics, you may choose to describe it here. For example, if you worked at an MRI lab but your primary responsibilities involved subject location, screening, and interviews, this would be an important descriptive detail to establish in this section.

Teaching Experience

Often this details: the institutions where you've taught, your job titles at these institutions (e.g., TA, intern, adjunct instructor, etc.), the names and course numbers for the classes you've taught, and the dates when you taught these or the number of terms you taught them.

Research Experience

If you've served as a research assistant in any capacity, this would be an appropriate section to identify that. Depending on your field and experience, you may choose to detail: the names of labs you've worked in, the names of PIs you've worked under, the titles of projects you've worked on and the nature of your contributions, and the dates of your involvement. It is appropriate to use vocabulary here that is familiar to your scholarly peers.

Administrative Experience

If you have leadership experience in your department, you will want to identify your role, the name of the program, the dates you served in this capacity, and perhaps a brief description of your responsibilities. While many CV items won't include descriptions, when accounting for your administrative experience, you may need to offer a sentence or a concise bulleted list in order to inform your readers of what you did within this position.

Publications

Include the titles, names of any co-authors, and publication information for your scholarly reviewed publications. Often publications are organized in reverse chronological order starting with your most recent publication. There are some very specific rules about how to describe manuscripts that are under consideration but not yet accepted or that are in press. Be sure to ask your faculty advisers for instruction about how to claim credit for work in progress without inflating your accomplishments.

Sometimes CV writers want to showcase other, slightly less academic publications (e.g. blog posts or creative writing). If you choose to do this, make sure you use subsection titles to provide clear distinctions between types of publications.

Presentations and Posters

Include the presentation or poster titles, names of any co–presenters, conferences, and dates for your scholarly presentations at conferences. If you have many of these to choose from, select only the most relevant or prestigious presentations to include in a given CV.

Grants, Fellowships, Honors, and Awards

Depending on how many of these you have to draw from, you might choose to break this into subsections. Mostly, this section is about acknowledging the accolades you've won and the competitive resources you've received. Include the names of the awards or grants and the date you received them. Here again, be strategic about what you include. If a grant you received is particularly prestigious or sizable, it can be appropriate to detail the amount received.

Service

CV readers want to know about your participation on committees, the ways you've contributed to the life of your department or other organizations, and the associated volunteer work you've done. In this section, include information (titles, organization names, dates) about this part of your academic experience.

Professional Affiliations

If you've been a member of a scholarly organization, include the titles of those organizations and the years of your membership.

Languages

Especially if it is relevant to your research or academic work, include any languages you know and the extent of your proficiency. If appropriate for your field, this might include foreign languages as well as computer languages.[1]

写作要求

你应该把履历分成栏目分明的各个部分，这样才能方便你的读者浏览全文并了解你具有的与这份工作相关的条件或资格。具体包含的部分应该取决于你的背景和你所申请的职位。一般情况下，"教育"后的部分已经有既定秩序。当然，也可以强调你对这个职位最大的优势。比如，如果你申请一个研究型大学的职位，你最好把你发表的作品放在履历的首位。如果你申请的职位主要涉及教学，就以你的教学经验部分开始你的履历。在下文中，我们会为你介绍最常见的履历栏目：

联系信息

这类信息应该出现在你的履历开头，包括你的姓名、电话号码、通信地址（工作或者私人的）和专业的电子邮箱地址。你可能想轻微地改变一下格式或字体以便引起读者的更多注意，但是不要过分花工夫在这上面。

学历

一般情况下，这部分紧挨着联系信息部分。像大部分履历中的学历一样，这部分通常以时间倒叙的方式呈现，这样一来，你最近或者最高的学位或者正在攻读的学位就会最先映入读者的眼帘。提供的信息包括学校名称、已授予的学位、研究领域、主修和辅修专业以及被授予学位的年份。这部分也可以包括你的毕业论文的题目或者硕士论文题目和你主要导师的名字。通常情况下，不要写上你的平均成绩，也不要提到任何关于你学士学位之前的信息。

---

[1] CV Writing Tips: An Introduction to Writing a CV. https://writing.wisc.edu/Handbook/CV.html

工作经历

这部分主要与你的学术型工作、兴趣和发展相关。在简历中你可以描述你的工作、技能和成就,然而这样的细节描述在履历中通常是不合适的。例如,阅读你履历的人清楚地了解教授一门基础化学课程和哲学入门课程意味着什么。当然,如果相关学者不了解你以前工作的岗位,你需要在履历中适当介绍。例如,如果你以前在核磁共振实验室工作,但是你主要的工作责任涉及学科定位、筛检和访谈,那么这类信息应该成为你这部分的重点描述对象。

教学经验

通常包含这些细节:你曾经工作的机构地址和名称、你在这些机构内的职称(例如,助教、实习生、兼职讲师,等等)、授课班级的名称和课程总量以及你授课起始和截止日期和你的授课学期数。

研究经验

如果你担任过任何机构的助理研究员,这个部分会清楚展现你的研究经验。根据你的研究领域和经验,你还应该写上这些细节:曾经工作过的实验室的名称、学术带头人的名字、研究项目的名称、学术贡献的性质,还有你参与研究的时间范围。在这一部分,你最好使用学术同行所熟悉的词汇。

管理经验

如果你在某部门有过领导经验,你应该清楚地说明你的职务、项目名称、这段任职的起始和截止日期,也许还可以简洁地描述一下你的责任。尽管很多的履历中不会有描述,但是当涉及你的管理经验时,你需要提供一句话或者几个项目符号列表以至于让你的读者了解你在这个职位上完成的工作。

出版物

这是包括题目、合著作者姓名、出版信息等反映你学术背景的出版物。通常这一部分按照时间倒序,以你最近的出版物开头。这里也有一些特殊的规则,关于怎样描述那些正在考虑出版的原稿,但是不要描述你未被出版社接受或者正在印刷的手稿。请务必询问你的导师,怎样肯定自己正在进行的工作,同时又不会夸大其词。

有时求职者想在履历中展示学术性不太强的出版物(比如:博客帖子或者创造性的文章),如果你选择这样做,就应该分段写作,以使不同类型的出版物之间有明显的区别。

演讲和海报

包括演讲和海报的标题、所有合作演讲者的姓名、会议名称和学术演讲的日期。如果你有很多可供选择,在履历中挑选出相关性最强和最享有名望的演讲。

补助金、奖学金、荣誉和奖励

根据你所获得补助金、奖学金、荣誉和奖励的数量多少，你应该对该部分进行分段阐释。大多数情况下，这部分内容体现你赢得的荣誉和获得的竞争资源。一定要写清楚补助金和奖励的名称及获得日期。重申一遍，在写这部分内容时要进行策略性的思考。如果你获得了著名或者大额的补助金，那你应该把具体金额写出来。

志愿服务

阅读你履历的人想了解你参加组织的情况、你通过何种方式对你所在部门或组织做出了贡献以及你做过的相关志愿者工作。这部分应当涉及相关的学术经历信息，包括学术名称、组织名称和日期。

社会兼职

如果你是一名学术组织的成员，这部分要包含这些组织的名称和你成为其会员的年限。

语言

如果你的研究或学术工作和语言相关，写下你知晓的所有语言种类和精通程度。如果语言与你的专业领域相关，就可能不仅仅是只涉及外语，还有计算机语言。

Case Studies 案例分析

ELISABETH L. MILLER

Department of Anthropology

University of Wisconsin-Madison

5240 Sewell Social Science Building

1180 Observatory Drive

Madison, WI, 53706

ACADEMIC APPOINTMENTS

Assistant Professor of English, University of Nevada, Reno, Fall 2016 —

EDUCATION

PhD Candidate in English, Program in Composition and Rhetoric, University of Wisconsin-Madison, August 2016

Dissertation: Writing after Aphasia: Toward an Embodied Theory of Literacy

Committee: Kate Vieira (chair), Morris Young, Christa Olson, Jim Brown, Jenell Johnson, and Heather Krug Distributed minor: The Body in Research and Practice, with courses in gender & women's studies, anthropology, and communication arts Research and teaching interests: literacy studies, community literacy, disability studies, and writing across the curriculum.

Master of Arts in English Literature and Language, Winona State University, May 2009

Thesis: "How's the body?": The Human Body in James Joyce's Ulysses

Bachelor of Arts in English Writing and Bachelor of Science in Business Administration, Winona State University, May 2007.

PUBLICATIONS

Articles

"Literate Misfitting: Disability Theory and a Socio-Material Approach to Literacy. " College English (forthcoming Sept. 2016)

...

Book Reviews

Jay Dolmage's Disability Rhetoric. Co-author, with Jenell Johnson. Rhetoric Society Quarterly. 44. 3 (May 2014): 296-298.

...

FELLOWSHIPS and GRANTS

Research

University of Wisconsin-Madison Chancellor's Dissertation Fellowship (Fall 2015)

...

Community Writing Projects

"Allied Drive Neighborhood Storytelling Project. " Humanities Exposed (HEX) Grant. (with Chris Earle). Center for Humanities, UW-Madison, 2013. ($1250)

...

AWARDS and HONORS

Joyce Melville Award for Outstanding Scholarly Writing, UW-Madison English Department, recipient, 2015, Essay: "Literate Mismatch: Aphasia, Bodyminds, and the Materials of Literacy. "

...

NATIONAL CONFERENCES

"What Works in Interdisciplinary WAC Faculty Development? Results from a Pilot Research Study. " International Writing across the Curriculum Conference. Ann Arbor, MI (June 2016).

...

UNIVERSITY TEACHING

...

WRITING PROGRAM ADMINISTRATION

...

SELECTED INVITED WORKSHOPS and PRESENTATIONS

...

ACADEMIC LEADERSHIP and SERVICE

...

WORKSHOPS ATTENDED

...

PROFESSIONAL WRITING and EDITING

...

PROFESSIONAL AFFILIATIONS

...

REFERENCES

XXX
Assistant Professor of English
University of Wisconsin-Madison
608-334-xxxx
XXX@wisc. edu

XXX
Director, Writing Across the Curriculum
Director, Writing Center
University of Wisconsin-Madison
608-263-xxxx
XXX@wisc. edu

...

（文献来源：CV Writing Tips, the Writing Center, University of Wisconsin-Madison, https://writing. wisc. edu/Handbook/PDF/SampleCV1. pdf. ）

Analysis

Due to the limit of space, it's unlikely to show the readers the entire information involved in a CV. This sample is just trying to cover the overall structure, with the necessary headings of each part and some substantial information ensuing some headings omitted. Generally, such parts as education, publication and awards are extremely important for a job-hunter, especially for those aiming at securing a job in university or research institutes.

Supplementary Readings 拓展阅读

Elizabeth Ann Hennessy

Curriculum vitae

Geography Department 910B Lancaster Street
University of North Carolina at Chapel Hill Durham, NC 27701
Saunders Hall, CB 3220 919-260-4864
Chapel Hill, NC 27599-3220

EDUCATION

PhD	University of North Carolina at Chapel Hill
	Geography (expected May 2014)
	Dissertation: On the Backs of Turtles: Conserving Evolution in the Galápagos Islands
	Committee: Wendy Wolford (Chair), John Pickles, Scott Kirsch, Lawrence Grossberg (Communication Studies), Margaret Wiener (Anthropology)
MA	University of North Carolina at Chapel Hill
	Geography, 2006—2010
	Thesis: Crisis in Nature's Eden: Governing Nature and Culture in the Galápagos Islands
BA	Miami University, Oxford, Ohio, 1997—2001
	Majors: International Studies (Latin America concentration); English (Journalism concentration)
	Study Abroad: Universidad Nacional Autónoma de Heredia, Costa Rica, 2000

FELLOWSHIPS, GRANTS, AND AWARDS	
2013	Dissertation Completion Fellowship, American Council of Learned Societies/ Mellon Foundation
2012	William Wilson Brown, Jr. Dissertation Fellowship, UNC-Chapel Hill Institute for Study of the Americas
...	

PUBLICATIONS

...

INVITED LECTURES

...

CONFERENCE PARTICIPATION

...

TEACHING EXPERIENCE

...

PROFESSIONAL SERVICE

...

LANGUAGES

...

PROFESSIONAL AFFILIATIONS

...

（文献来源：CV Writing Tips, the Writing Center, University of Wisconsin-Madison, https://writing. wisc. edu/Handbook/PDF/SampleCV3. pdf. ）

Reading Comprehension

1. Compare this CV and the one in the section of Case Studies, what are the similarities between the two?
2. What are the features of this one?
3. Is there anything that needs to be improved?

Exercise
课后练习

● True or False

Directions: Read the following sentences and decide whether they are true or false.

1. Resume is only 1 page and absolutely no longer than 2 pages, while CV can be kept as long as you need.
2. Resume is used in a more academic way than CV.
3. Not only your academic work should be involved in CV, but other work experiences are as important as academic one included in CV.

● Gap–Filling

Directions: Complete each sentence with appropriate words.

1. Contact information of a resume should be at the top of your page and include your _____, your _____, your _____, and your _____.
2. While you may choose to not use subsections and there may be others to consider, the three most common are: _____ experience, _____ experience, and _____ experience.

● Short Answer Questions

Directions: Answer the following questions briefly.

1. What are the most important points of comparison and contrast between resume and CV needed to be aware of?
2. As the crucial part of your resume, what kind of work experience do you need to pay much attention to?

● Simulative Exercise

Based on your understanding of the purpose and requirement of resume and CV, try to write a resume or a CV.

Note Making
笔记

Abstract 内容概览

Note-making is a process that involves writing or recording what you hear or read in a descriptive way. This is often the first stage of the process of producing effective notes.

Developing your own effective note making strategies can help you to actively engage with your learning. This chapter will help you to reflect on your current approach to taking and making notes, and suggest techniques for making your notes more meaningful and useful.

笔记是一种通过描写的方式，把你所听所读的东西记录下来的过程。这是有效笔记产生过程的第一阶段。

训练有效做笔记的方法能帮助你积极地投入到学习中。这一章将会帮你审视现有做笔记方法的不足之处，并提供建设性技巧，使你的笔记更为高效有用。

Basic Knowledge 基础知识

Introduction

Note-making is an advanced process that involves reviewing, synthesizing, connecting ideas from the lecture or reading and presenting the information in a readable, creative way that will stick in your mind.

A successful note should contain the following elements:

- Source: e.g.title of lecture/book/article, date, etc.
- Headings: capturing key topics
- Keywords: key points, examples, illustrations, names, new ideas
- Mnemonic triggers: things that make your notes memorable such as cartoons, colour, etc.
- Further reading: people or articles to read, noted and highligted[①]

简介

记笔记是一个复杂的用脑过程,包括复习、整合、联系与讲座和阅读有关的观点以及通过可读的和富有创造性的方式将头脑中的信息呈现出来。

成功的笔记应该包含如下几个要素:
- 来源:例如讲座、书籍以及文章的题目、日期,等等
- 标题:抓住关键话题
- 关键词:关键点、例子、说明、名称、新观点
- 触发记忆的因素:一些能使你笔记难忘的事物,比如卡通动画、颜色,等等
- 拓展阅读:下一步的阅读材料,记得做笔记并突出重点

Writing Requirement

1. Before you even start, make a note of your source(s). If this is a book, an article, or a journal, write the following information at the head of your notes: Author, title, publisher, publication date, and edition of book.

2. Use loose-leaf A4 paper. This is now the international standard for almost all printed matter. Don't use small notepads. You will find it easier to keep track of your notes if they fit easily alongside your other study materials.

3. Write clearly and leave a space between each note. Don't try to cram as much as possible onto one page. Keeping the items separate will make them easier to recall. The act of laying out information in this way will cause you to assess the importance of each detail.

4. Use some system of tabulation. This will help to keep the items separate from

---

① Burns, T. and Sinfeld, S. *Essential Study Skills: the Complete Guide to Success at University*. Los Angeles: Sage, 2008.

each other. Even if the progression of numbers doesn't mean a great deal, it will help you to keep the items distinct.

5. Don't attempt to write continuous prose. Notes should be abbreviated and compressed. Full grammatical sentences are not necessary. Use abbreviations, initials, and shortened forms of commonly used terms.

6. Don't string the points together continuously, one after the other on the page. You will find it very difficult to untangle these items from each other after some time has passed.

7. Devise a logical and a memorable layout. Use lettering, numbering, and indentation for sections and for sub-sections. Use headings and sub-headings. Good layout will help you to absorb and recall information. Some people use coloured inks and highligters to assist this process of identification.

8. Use a new page for each set of notes. This will help you to store and identify them later. Keep topics separate, and have them clearly titled and labeled to facilitate easy recall.

9. Write on one side of the page only. Number these pages. Leave the blank sides free for possible future additions, and for any details which may be needed later.[1]

Meanwhile, in order to make your notes effective, you need to

- Use headings, underlining and capitals to organize the notes on the page
- Use symbols/abbreviations for brevity
- Use bullets or numbering
- Leave good margins so you can add additional notes, thoughts or questions
- Use "quotation marks" to show direct quotes from your lectures or the source you are using
- Identify where you have noted your own ideas, e.g. use [square brackets]

After you have made your notes you need to ensure that you do something with them. You should

- Label and file your notes (physically or online)
- Cross reference them with any handouts
- Read through your notes and fill in any details from your additional reading or research

---

[1] Vladimir Naumets, Summary Writing Guidelines, https://www. academia. edu/4607842/Summary_Writing_GUIDELINES

- Link new information to what you already know
- Discuss with others, compare, fill in gaps.

写作要求

1. 在你记笔记之前，写下你的信息来源。如果对象是书、文章或者期刊，你需要在你的笔记开头记录以下信息：作者、标题、出版者、出版日期和书籍版本。

2. 使用 A4 的活页纸。这是现在几乎所有印刷品的国际标准。不要使用小的笔记本。如果笔记的大小很符合其他研究材料的尺寸，你会发现做笔记更简单容易。

3. 字迹清晰，笔记之间留出空白。不要在一页上记得密密麻麻，保持笔记之间的必要间隙会让你更容易回忆起相关细节。用这种方法记录、安排笔记能使你衡量每个细节的重要性。

4. 使用表格。这会使你的每个项目相互隔开，明晰可辨。

5. 不要企图写出连续性的散文。笔记应该是缩写和简写的，没必要使用语法完整的句子。使用缩写词、首字母和常见短语的简写形式和符号。

6. 不要把每个要点一个接一个、成串连续写在一起。一段时间之后，你会发现整理这些笔记很棘手。

7. 设计一个有逻辑性、便于记忆的笔记布局。使用字母、数字、缩进处理每个部分。最好使用标题和副标题。这些设计会帮助你消化和记忆相关信息。有些人会借助不同颜色的墨水和荧光笔来区分重点。

8. 每次做笔记都要用新的一页记录。这会帮助你之后的记忆和区分。不同的话题要隔开，并且给它们加上清楚的题目和标签来帮助记忆。

9. 单面记录，并给页码编号。留出空白面为以后可能进行补充或者添加任何有必要的细节做准备。

  与此同时，一份有效的笔记还需要：
- 使用标题、下画线、大写字母来组织你的笔记
- 使用符号和缩略词
- 使用项目符号或编号
- 适当留白，以便增添额外的笔记、想法和疑问
- 使用引号来表示你从授课中直接引用的原话或者使用的文献来源
- 能分辨出哪里是你自己思想和观点，比如使用［方括号］

在你做好笔记之后,你需要整理这些笔记,包括:
- 标注你做的笔记并将其整理归类(纸质版或电子版)
- 和讲义资料进行对照参考
- 通读你的笔记,并增添你额外阅读和研究的内容
- 把新知识和已知的信息相结合
- 和其他人进行讨论和对比,以便查漏补缺。

Case Studies
案例分析

Cornell Notes

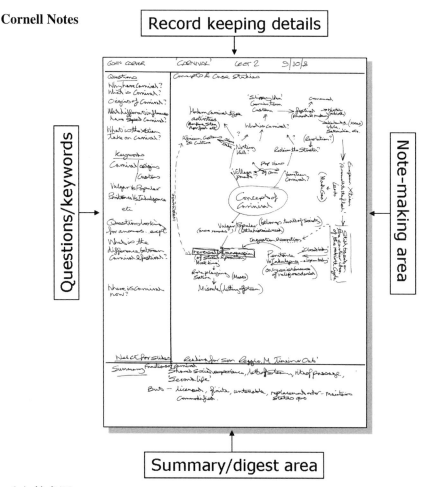

(文献来源:Student Learning Advisory Service, University of Kent, https://www.kent.ac.uk/learning/resources/studyguides/notemaking.pdf.)

Analysis

The Cornell note-taking system is one of the most popular and effective ways of making notes for college students. The note-making and record keeping areas are filled-in during the note-making activity time, and the summary/digest and questions/keywords areas completed later on during reflection. (NB. use A3 size paper to ensure sufficient space for recording information; if this isn't enough room, then you're probably noting down too much information.)

Supplementary Readings
拓展阅读

What follows is an example of notes taken whilst listening to an Open University radio broadcast — a half hour lecture by the philosopher and cultural historian, Isaiah Berlin. It was entitled "Tolstoy's Views on Art and Morality", which was part of the third level course in literary studies A 312 — The Nineteenth Century Novel and its Legacy.

Isaiah Berlin — "Tolstoy on Art and Morality" — 3 Sep 89

1. T's views on A extreme — but he asks important questions which disturb society

2. 1840s Univ of Kazan debate on purpose of A

T believes there should be simple answers to probs of life

3. Met simple & spontaneous people & soldiers in Caucasus

Crimean Sketches admired by Turgenev & Muscovites but T didn't fit in milieu

4. Westernizers Vs Slavophiles — T agreed with Ws

but rejects science (Ss romantic conservatives)

5. 2 views of A in mid 19C — A for art's sake/ A for society's sake

6. Pierre (W&P) and Levin (AK) as egs of "searchers for truth"

7. Natural life (even drunken violence) better than intellectual

8. T's contradiction — to be artist or moralist

9. T's 4 criteria for work of art

know what you want to say — lucidly and clearly
subject matter must be of essential interest
artist must live or imagine concretely his material
A must know the moral centre of situation
10. T crit of other writers

Shkspre and Goethe — too complex
St Julien (Flaubert) inauthentic
Turgenev and Chekhov guilty of triviality
11. What is Art? Emotion recollected and transmitted to others

[Wordsworth] Not self-expression — Only good should be transmitted

12. But his own tastes were for high art

Chopin, Beethoven, & Mozart

T Argues he himself corrupted

13. Tried to distinguish between his own art and moral tracts

> 14. "Artist cannot help burning like a flame"
>
> 15. Couldn't reconcile contradictions in his own beliefs
>
> Died still raging against self and society

（文献来源：Roy Johnson, Revision and Examinations: Guidance Notes for Students, Manchester: Clifton Press, 1993, p.17.）

Reading Comprehension

1. What is the type of note-making?

2. How do you evaluate this sample note-making?

3. Can you come up with some ways to improve this note-making?

Exercise
课后练习

● True or False

Directions: Read the following sentences and decide whether they are true or false.

1. A successful note should contain five elements: source, headings, keywords, mnemonic triggers, further reading.

2. You can use small notepads as much as possible instead of loose-leaf A4 paper.

3. You'd better string the points together continuously, one after the other on the page, in order to reduce the waste of papers.

● Gap-Filling

Directions: Complete each sentence with appropriate words.

1. Don't attempt to write continuous prose. Notes should be _____ and _____.

2. Devise a _____ and a _____ layout. Use lettering, numbering, and indentation for sections and for sub-sections.

笔记 | Note Making

● Short Answer Questions

Directions: Answer the following questions briefly.

1. What are the essential elements of compressed notes?
2. What should you do to polish the notes you take in class?

● Simulative Exercise

Do a self-exercising of note making with these new methods based on your understanding and learning of requirements of note making.

Part Two　Business Writing

第二部分　商务写作

Business Writing Style
商务写作概述

Abstract 内容概览

One of the keys to the success of a business is effective communication. A business's employees and other in-house players can only get on well and work together to spur the business to success when there's effective communication between them. Similarly, a business can only build positive relationships with customers using effective communication.

Now, since writing is one of the commonest and most important means of communication in the business world, it goes without saying that business writing skills are more than important to the success of a business.[①]

商业成功的关键之一在于有效沟通。企业的雇员和员工只有在有效沟通时，才能顺利开展工作，共同推动企业取得成功。同样，企业只能通过有效的沟通与客户建立积极的合作关系。

现如今，自从写作成为商务交流最为普遍和最为重要的方式之一，商务写作技能自然对于企业的成功发挥着极其重要的作用。

The Purposes of Business Writing 商业写作目的

1. Business writing skills foster effective communication

Writing alone makes it possible for a business to communicate with its players

---

① http://www.mytopbusinessideas.com/why-writing-skills-important/

and stakeholders through a wide range of channels. These include emails, reports, company brochures, presentations, sales materials, visual aids, Case Studies, social media updates, and so on. All these pieces must be written in a professional, comprehensive, and informative way, yet easy to read and comprehend. Only effective business writing skills can make this possible.

2. Business writing skills boost credibility

When a business is able to effectively communicate to its potential customers in clear, simple, yet professional language, such a business will most likely win more customers. This is because flawless writing sends signals of diligence and quality. Poor writing, on the other hand, destroys a business's reputation quickly. Potential customers see businesses with poorly written promotional materials as unprofessional.

3. Business writing skills help to keep records

Writing is the best way to keep information for the long term. Information shared through verbal communication is lost almost immediately after the presentation. But information presented in written form can be kept for years, without any bit of it getting lost. This explains why the most accurate pieces of information that has reached us from hundreds of years back are those preserved in books.

4. Business writing skills create opportunities

Businesses need to grab opportunities as they come. They need to contact potential customers frequently. They need to send proposals. They need to advertise their products and services. And they need to send written proposals if there exists a business project or opportunity. With business writing skills that are stellar, businesses can accomplish all of these, thereby creating huge opportunities for themselves in the short and long terms.[①]

---

① http://www. mytopbusinessideas. com/why-writing-skills-important/

商务写作概述 | Business Writing Style

1. 商务写作技巧可促进有效交流

仅仅通过商务写作就可能让商务参与者和利益相关者们通过各种各样的渠道进行商务交流。这些渠道包括电子邮件、报告、公司手册、演示文稿、销售材料、视觉辅助、案例研究、社交媒体的更新，等等。所有这些作品必须以专业、全面和翔实的方式写成，同时要易于阅读和理解。只有借助于有效的商务写作技巧才能使之成为可能。

2. 商务写作技巧能增强可信度

在商业贸易中，如果能用清楚、简单却不乏专业性的语言跟潜在客户进行有效的交流，这样的交易大部分都会赢得更多的客户。这是因为完美的写作会给人勤奋、严谨、高质量的印象，而劣质的写作会很快对公司的声誉造成恶劣的影响。潜在客户会认为质量低下的商务营销写作是不专业的。

3. 商务写作技巧有助于保存记录

写作是长期保存信息的最好方式。通过口头言语分享的信息在陈述展示后，几乎很快就会被遗忘。但以书面形式提供的信息可以保存多年，不会有任何丢失。这就解释了为什么我们能够知晓的数千百年前的准确信息大多都是通过书本保存下来的。

4. 商务写作技巧能创造更多机会

商人需要在机会来临时抢占先机。他们需要频繁地跟潜在客户取得联系、发送提案并为自己的产品和服务打广告。如果确实存在一个商业项目和机会，他们必须发送已写好的提案。如果这个公司的商务写作水平一流，他们就能完成以上所有的事宜，为自己创造短期或长期的巨大商机。

The Requirements of Business Writing
商务写作要求

What does effective business writing look like? The following characteristics are especially important for business writing.

1. Clear Purpose

The well-known saying, "Time is money," is well-known because it's true. Nobody—especially a business person—wants his time wasted, so be sure your purpose is clear and that what you write is worth taking the time to read.

2. Clarity and Conciseness

There is a time and a place for creative figures of speech and poetic turns of phrase, but rarely is a business letter that time or place. The priority in business writing is the effective communication of specific information. Avoid wasting words and be precise with the ones you choose.

3. Awareness of Audience

Know the audience you are writing to. It makes a difference whether you are communicating with a customer service representative, a long-time co-worker, or a potential new client. Beware of phrases and expressions that could be misunderstood or offensive. Know what your reader needs and wants to hear, and allow that knowledge to shape your writing.

4. Appropriate Tone

One tricky aspect of writing is that tone (i.e. , the attitude of the writer toward his subject or audience) can easily be misinterpreted. Pay attention not only to what is said, but how your words may be interpreted. Do not be overly informal or familiar.

5. Attention to Form

Business letters, proposals, memos, and many other types of business writing require particular formats. Adhering to standard form eliminates confusion and helps the reader quickly identify the purpose of the document. Attention to details of form is more important in business writing than most other kinds of writing.

In many ways writing in a business setting is less demanding than other kinds of writing. There is little pressure to be creative or particularly original. You are not creating art, after all; you are using the written word for its most basic purpose:

to communicate information. This, however, is not always as simple as you might think. Good business writing, like every skill, requires practice.①

有效的商务写作有什么具体要求呢？以下是商务写作必不可少的几个特征。

1. 目标明确

俗话说："时间就是金钱"。没有任何一个人——尤其是一个商务人员——愿意浪费他的时间，因此你需要保证你的目标明确，并且你所写的东西值得花时间去阅读。

2. 清晰简洁

在具有创造性特征的演讲和诗意转折的短语中，时间和地点是必要的，但在商业信函中几乎不需要具体的时间和地点。商务写作的优先事项是具体信息的有效沟通，避免浪费话语，并准确地选择你的用词。

3. 知彼意识

了解你的读者群。分辨你交流的对象是客户服务代表、长期合伙人还是潜在新客户，你的写作会因此有所不同。注意可能会造成误解或看起来有侵犯性的短语和表达。清楚你的客户需要什么、想听到什么，并根据这些要求来设计你的写作以满足不同类型客户需要。

4. 口吻得体

另外一个关于商务写作的棘手问题就是口吻（比如作者对话题和读者的态度）容易被误解。切忌讽刺。不仅要关注你写的内容，更要注意读者的解读方式。千万不要过分随意或者太过口语化。

5. 注意格式

商业信函、提案、备忘录以及很多其他类型的商务写作都需要特定的格式。坚持标准格式能排除很多的疑惑、混淆，也能帮助读者快速辨别文件的目的所在。相较于其他写作类型来说，商务写作更注意写作格式的细节。

在大多数情况中，商务写作没有其他写作类型的要求高，因为商务写作几

---

① https://www.pinterest.com/pin/207376757812964611/

乎没有创新的压力，特别是原创的压力。毕竟，你不是艺术创作者，你是在用写作语言表达你最基本的目的：交流信息。然而，它也并不如你想得过于简单。优秀的商务写作也像其他技术一样，需要勤加练习。

Exercise 课后练习

● **True or False**

Directions: Read the following sentences and decide whether they are true or false.

1. Now, though writing is one of the commonest and most important means of communication in the business world, it does not mean that business writing skills are more than important to the success of a business.
2. Flawless writing sends signals of diligence and quality, while poor writing destroys a business's reputation quickly.
3. There is little pressure to be creative or particularly original, so it is very simple to do with business writing.

● **Gap-Filling**

Directions: Complete each sentence with appropriate words.

1. These include emails, reports, company brochures, presentations, sales materials, visual aids, Case Studies, social media updates, and so on. All these pieces must be written in a _____, _____ and _____ way, yet easy to read and comprehend.
2. Business letters, proposals, memos, and many other types of business writing require particular formats. Adhering to standard form _____ confusion and helps the reader quickly _____ the purpose of the document.

● **Short Answer Questions**

Directions: Answer the following questions briefly.

1. What're the functions of good business writing skills?
2. What need you pay attention to in order to produce a good and effective business writing?

商务写作概述 | Business Writing Style

● **Simulative Exercise**

Suppose now you are addressing a couple of employees who are eager to know the basic skills of business writing, what would you say to them?

Memo
备忘录

Abstract
内容概览

  Memos have a twofold purpose: they bring attention to problems and they solve problems. They accomplish their goals by informing the reader about new information like policy changes, price increases, or by persuading the reader to take an action, such as attend a meeting, or change a current production procedure. Regardless of the specific goal, memos are most effective when they connect the purpose of the writer with the interests and needs of the reader.

  Choose the audience of the memo wisely. Ensure that all of the people that the memo is addressed to need to read the memo. If it is an issue involving only one person, do not send the memo to the entire office. Also, be certain that material is not too sensitive to put in a memo; sometimes the best forms of communication are face-to-face interaction or a phone call. Memos are most effectively used when sent to a small number of people to communicate company or job objectives.

  备忘录有两个目的：注意问题，解决问题。通过向读者通报政策变化、价格上涨等新信息，或通过说服读者采取行动，如参加会议或改变当前的生产程序来实现目标。无论具体的目标是什么，当需要把作者的目的与读者的利益和需求联系起来的时候，备忘录是最有效的途径。

  明智地选择备忘录的受众群。确保接收备忘录的所有人都需要阅读它。如果是只涉及一个人，则不要将备忘录发送给所有办公室人员。而且，要保证写进备忘录的材料不能太敏感，有时最好的交流方式是面对面互动或电话沟通。在向少数人发送公司目标或工作目标时，使用备忘录是最有效的途径。

备忘录 | Memo

Basic Knowledge
基础知识

Introduction

A memorandum or memo helps members of an organization communicate and share information that is relevant to people within the organization. While business letters allow members of an organization communicate with people outside the organization, memos usually contain information that affects those within a particular organization. They allow members or departments within an organization to communicate and relay information. Memos frequently address a small or large group of people, but some of the memos you write may be intended for one person.

Memos often share new information, like changes to schedules or benefits, or they may encourage the reader to take an action, such as attend a meeting or use less paper. Your aim in writing a memo is the same as with other professional correspondence: You want to quickly and effectively communicate your purpose to your reader.

When preparing to write a memo, ask yourself the following questions:

- What is the purpose of the memo? What will it tell its recipient(s)?
- Why do the recipients need this information?
- What are the most important facts that the recipients need to have?
- Is there a change that will be occurring? If so, what is the change and when will it occur?
- Is there an action that the recipients need to take? If so, exactly what do they need to do? How do they take this action?
- Is there any information (contact names, numbers, URLs) they need to have in order take this action?
- Is there any accompanying documentation (reports, forms, charts) that the recipients need? (These can be included as attachments to the memo.)
- Why do the recipients need to take the action? What are the benefits? How will it affect them?

The text of the memo should be relatively short; one page is a good rule of thumb. While you don't want to omit any information that the reader needs, it's also important to keep explanations short and simple. This will increase the likelihood of getting your point across, because most people will read a short, concise memo right away. Discuss only what the reader needs to know, but include information about where to obtain additional information if necessary.①

简介

  一份备忘录能帮助一个组织的成员沟通和分享信息。虽然商业信函有助于组织成员与组织之外的人进行沟通，但备忘录通常包含影响特定组织内部人员的信息。他们主要帮助组织内的成员或部门沟通和传递信息。备忘录经常涉及一小群人或一大批人，但某些备忘录也可能是针对一个人的。

  备忘录经常分享新的信息，比如时间表或收益的变动，或者鼓励读者采取行动，比如参加会议或少用纸张。写备忘录的目的和其他专业信函一样：快速有效地将你的目的传达给你的读者。

  当你准备写一份备忘录的时候，请问自己如下几个问题：

1. 写此份备忘录的目的是什么？它将传递给接收者怎样的信息？
2. 接收者为何需要这个信息？
3. 接收者需要接收的最重要的事实是什么？
4. 还会发生变动吗？如果有，那么变动是什么，它何时会发生？
5. 为了采取某个行动，接收者需要掌握什么信息吗？（包含名称、数量、链接）
6. 接收者需要什么相关文件吗？（如报告、表格、图表）（这些可作为备忘录的附件）
7. 接收者为什么要执行这项行动？好处是什么？这将给他们带来怎样的影响？

  备忘录的文本应相对较短；控制在一页内是一个很好的经验法则。虽然你并不想省略读者需要的任何信息，保持简洁的说明也同样重要。这将增加你传达出自己的观点的机会，因为大多数人会首先读一份简洁的备忘录。你只需传达出读者需要知道的内容，但是，如果有必要的话，也可包含何处可获得更多资料的信息。

---

① Memos: Get advice on writing effective memos, https://www.umuc.edu/current-students/learning-resources/writing-center/writing-resources/memos/

Writing Requirement

Parts of a Memo

Standard memos are divided into segments to organize the information and to help achieve the writer's purpose.

Heading Segment

The heading segment follows this general format:

TO: (readers' names and job titles)

FROM: (your name and job title)

DATE: (complete and current date)

SUBJECT: (what the memo is about, highlighted in some way)

Make sure you address the reader by his or her correct name and job title. You might call the company president "Maxi" on the golf course or in an informal note, but "Rita Maxwell, President" would be more appropriate for a formal memo. Be specific and concise in your subject line. For example, "Clothes" as a subject line could mean anything from a dress code update to a production issue. Instead use something like, "Fall Clothes Line Promotion".

Opening Segment

The purpose of a memo is usually found in the opening paragraph and includes: the purpose of the memo, the context and problem, and the specific assignment or task. Before indulging the reader with details and the context, give the reader a brief overview of what the memo will be about. Choosing how specific your introduction will be depends on your memo plan style. The more direct the memo plan, the more explicit the introduction should be. Including the purpose of the memo will help clarify the reason the audience should read this document. The introduction should be brief, and should be approximately the length of a short paragraph.

Context

The context is the event, circumstance, or background of the problem you are solving. You may use a paragraph or a few sentences to establish the background and state the problem. Oftentimes it is sufficient to use the opening of a sentence to completely explain the context, such as,

"Through market research and analysis..."

Include only what your reader needs, but be sure it is clear.

Task Segment

One essential portion of a memo is the task statement where you should describe what you are doing to help solve the problem. If the action was requested, your task may be indicated by a sentence opening like,

"You asked that I look at..."

If you want to explain your intentions, you might say,

"To determine the best method of promoting the new fall line, I will..."

Include only as much information as is needed by the decision-makers in the context, but be convincing that a real problem exists. Do not ramble on with insignificant details. If you are having trouble putting the task into words, consider whether you have clarified the situation. You may need to do more planning before you're ready to write your memo. Make sure your purpose-statement forecast divides your subject into the most important topics that the decision-maker needs.

Summary Segment

If your memo is longer than a page, you may want to include a separate summary segment. However, this section not necessary for short memos and should not take up a significant amount of space. This segment provides a brief statement of the key recommendations you have reached. These will help your reader understand the key points of the memo immediately. This segment may also include references to methods and sources you have used in your research.

Discussion Segments

The discussion segments are the longest portions of the memo, and are the parts in which you include all the details that support your ideas. Begin with the information that is most important. This may mean that you will start with key findings or recommendations. Start with your most general information and move to your specific or supporting facts. (Be sure to use the same format when including details: strongest to weakest.) The discussion segments include the supporting ideas, facts and research that back up your argument in the memo. Include strong points and evidence to persuade the reader to follow your recommended actions. If this section is inadequate, the memo will not be as effective as it could be.

Closing Segment

After the reader has absorbed all of your information, you want to close with a courteous ending that states what action you want your reader to take. Make sure you consider how the reader will benefit from the desired actions and how you can make those actions easier. For example, you might say,

"I will be glad to discuss this recommendation with you during our Tuesday trip to the spa and follow through on any decisions you make."

Necessary Attachments

Make sure you document your findings or provide detailed information whenever necessary. You can do this by attaching lists, graphs, tables, etc. at the end of your memo. Be sure to refer to your attachments in your memo and add a notation about what is attached below your closing, like this:

Attached: Focus Group Results, January- May 2007

Format

The format of a memo follows the general guidelines of business writing. A memo is usually a page or two long, should be single spaced and left justified. Instead of using indentations to show new paragraphs, skip a line between sentences. Business materials should be concise and easy to read. Therefore it is beneficial to use headings and lists to help the reader pinpoint certain information.

You can help your reader understand your memo better by using headings for the summary and the discussion segments that follow it. Write headings that are short but that clarify the content of the segment. For example, instead of using "Summary" for your heading, try "New Advertising Recommendations", which is much more specific. The major headings you choose are the ones that should be incorporated in your purpose-statement in the opening paragraph.

For easy reading, put important points or details into lists rather than paragraphs when possible. This will draw the readers' attention to the section and help the audience remember the information better. Using lists will help you be concise when writing a memo.

The segments of the memo should be allocated in the following manner:

Header: 1/8 of the memo

Opening, Context and Task: 1/4 of the memo

Summary, Discussion Segment: 1/2 of the memo

Closing Segment, Necessary Attachments: 1/8 of the memo

This is a suggested distribution of the material to make writing memos easier. Not all memos will be the same and the structure can change as you see necessary.

Different organizations may have different formatting procedures, so be flexible in adapting your writing skills.[①]

写作要求

备忘录的组成
一份标准的备忘录可分为组成信息的部分和帮助作者实现目标的部分。

标题部分
标题部分遵循如下通用格式：
TO：（读者的姓名和职称）
FROM：（作者的姓名和职称）
DATE：（完整的当天日期）
SUBJECT：（这份备忘录是关于什么的，用某种方式强调说明）

确保以正确的名字和职务名称来称呼你的读者。当你和你的总裁打高尔夫球时，或者在一份非正式笔记里，你也许会叫他"马克西"，但是在一份正式的备忘录里，称他为"总裁瑞塔·麦克斯维尔先生"则是更为恰当的方式。你的主题应该具体且简洁。比如，用"衣服"作为主题，可能包含从服装代码更新到生产的各项问题。可以用诸如"秋季服装生产线的推广"来代之。

开头部分
备忘录的目的通常出现在开头的段落中，它包括：备忘录的目的、背景和问题，以及具体的任务。在读者阅读细节之前，应先给读者简单介绍一下备忘录的内容。介绍的详略取决于备忘录的风格。备忘录的计划越直接，介绍的内容就应越明确。介绍备忘录的目的有助于阐明读者阅读这份文件的原因。引言应该简短，大致相当于一个短段落的长度。

情况说明
情况说明是你所解决问题的事件、情况或背景。你可以用一个段落或几句话来说明背景和陈述问题。通常，句子的开头就可以说明情况，如"通过市场调研和分析……"

仅包括读者需要知晓的内容，但要确保其清晰明了。

任务部分
任务部分是备忘录的一个主要部分，你需要讲明为了帮助解决这个问题，你在做什么。如果需要采取某个行动，任务部分的开头句可以表示为："你要

---

① https://owl.english.purdue.edu/owl/resource/590/03/

求我着眼于……"

如果你想解释你的意向，你也可以说："为了确定推广新的秋季生产线的最佳方案，我将……"

内容仅包括决策者所需的信息，但是也要标明真正存在的问题。不要过多赘述无关紧要的细节。如果你在将任务转化为文字的步骤上存在困难，则需要思考一下你是否清楚地阐明了形势。在做好写备忘录的准备之前，你可能需要做更详尽的规划。确保让你的目的陈述将主题分割成决策者所需的几个最为重要的论题。

总结部分

如果你的备忘录长度超过一页，或许你可以把它归纳为几个独立的部分。然而，对一个简短的备忘录来说，这一步骤并不是必需的，因此不应占用大量空间。此部分是你所提出的主要建议的简要介绍。它将帮助你的读者快速理解备忘录中的主要观点。这一部分还可能包括在你的调查中所使用到的引用部分及其来源。

讨论部分

讨论部分是备忘录中最长的部分，也是包含所有支持你想法的细节的部分。从最重要的信息着手，这可能意味着你将从关键的发现或建议开始。从最基本的信息开始，继而转移到具体的论据（要确保在描述细节时使用相同的格式：由最强的到最弱的）。在备忘录中，讨论部分包括支撑你论点的分论点、事实和调查研究。利用有力的论点和证据来说服读者遵循你的建议。如果这个部分不充分，备忘录将不会完全发挥它的效用。

结尾部分

在读者知晓了所有信息之后，你应该以一个礼貌的结尾来结束那些关于你想让你的读者采取何种行动的陈述。要确保你考虑了读者将如何从所期望的行动中获益，以及如何使这些行动变得更容易。例如，你可能会说"我很高兴在周二的 spa 之旅中与你讨论这一建议，并全力支持你做出的任何决定"。

必要附件

确保在任何必要的时候能用文件证明你的发现或者提供细节信息。你可在备忘录的最后附上列表、图表、表格等。在你的备忘录中，一定要提到你的附件，并在结尾加以标记，如：Attached: Focus Group Results, January-May 2007。

格式

备忘录的格式遵循商务写作的一般准则。一份备忘录通常是一页或两页，应该使用单倍行距和左对齐。不要使用缩进来表明这是新的段落，而是另起一行。商务材料应该简明易懂。因此,使用标题和列表来帮助读者精确定位某些信息是不错的选择。

在摘要的部分以及随后的讨论部分使用标题,可以帮助读者更好地理解你的备忘录。标题要短,但也要能够阐明此部分的内容。例如,不要用"摘要"来代替你的标题,试试更为具体的"新的广告推荐"。你所选择的主要标题应该出现在开头段落的目的陈述部分。

为了便于阅读,在可能的情况下,把重点或细节放在列表中,而不是段落当中。这能吸引读者对此部分的关注,帮助他们更好地记住信息。并且,使用列表可以帮助你的备忘录更加简洁。

备忘录各部分的详略可参考以下的分配方案:

1. 标题:整篇备忘录的八分之一。
2. 开头、背景及任务部分:整篇备忘录的四分之一。
3. 总结、讨论部分:整篇备忘录的二分之一。
4. 结尾部分及必要附件:整篇备忘录的八分之一。

这种分配方案能让你的备忘录写作变得更加容易,但并不是所有的备忘录都要遵循同样标准,可以根据你的需要改变备忘录的结构。不同的组织可能会有不同的格式要求,因此请灵活调整你的写作技巧。

Case Studies
案例分析

Sample Memo

TO: Gaby Duane
FROM: Clark Thomas
RE: Loman's Fashions - Breach of contract claim (advertising circular)
DATE: April 26, 2002

QUESTION PRESENTED [1]
Under New York law, did Loman's Fashions' description of a designer leather coat in an advertising circular constitute an offer to sell the coat which

became a binding contract when the text of the advertisement indicated that the coats were a "manufacturer's closeout" and that the early shopper would be rewarded, and when a shopper signified her intent to purchase the coat according to the advertised terms?

SHORT ANSWER 2

No. Where, as here, the text of the advertisement merely stated that the sale was a "manufacturer's closeout" and that the "early" shopper would "catch the savings", the advertisement was not an offer to sell the coat which could be converted into a binding contract by conduct signifying an acceptance of the advertised terms.

FACTS 3

Loman's Fashions, a retailer of women's and men's outerwear, distributed a circular in November advertising a manufacturer's closeout of designer women's leather coats for $59. 99, coats that regularly sold for $300. 00. The ad announced that the store would open at 7a.m. on Friday, November 30, and stated that the "early bird catches the savings!" After about fifteen minutes, all the advertised coats had been sold. At 7:30 a.m. , a shopper inquired about the coats and was told that there were none left, but she complained that Loman's was obligated to sell her a comparably valued designer leather coat at the advertised price. The store manager declined, and the shopper filed a complaint in Small Claims Court, alleging that Loman's had breached a contract by failing to sell the advertised leather coats at the advertised price.

Loman's president, WilliLoman, stated that the store occasionally gives rain checks when it is possible to replenish supplies of an item that Loman's can purchase at a discount. In this case, the manufacturer had discontinued the line of coats and Loman's was not prepared to sell other, designer leather coats at such a drastic markdown. Loman expressed concern that, if the shopper's interpretation were to hold, Loman's would have to reconsider its marketing strategies; she had assumed that the advertised terms applied while supplies lasted. She asks whether Loman's would have any contractual obligation under

> these circumstances.
>
> ...
>
> CONCLUSION [4]
> On these facts, the court will probably find that the claimant has failed to state a cause of action for breach of contract because the ad did not constitute an offer but merely an invitation to negotiate.

（文献来源：Drafting a Law Office Memorandum, CUNY School of Law, http://www.law.cuny.edu/legal-writing/students/memorandum/memorandum-3.html.）

Analysis

1) The question presented states the question(s) the memo is to address: how does the relevant law apply to the key facts of the research problem? The question should be sufficiently narrow and should be objective.

2) The short answer contains a clear answer to the question (i.e., a prediction) and an explanation of that answer. The balanced description of law and fact that you provide in the question presented should be mirrored in the short answer.

The short answer serves two functions: (i) it provides hurried readers with an accessible, bottom-line prediction as well as the core of the relevant law and facts; and (ii) it provides the more thorough readers with an outline or digest of your subsequent discussion section. The short answer should function as a roadmap to help readers feel oriented when they move on to the discussion.

3) The facts section contains all the factual premises upon which your subsequent legal analysis is based. Certainly, all the facts cited in the application section (The "A" in IRAC or CRRACC) of your discussion should be presented as part of the story told in the facts section.

Bear in mind that the busy law-trained reader will value conciseness in this section, so try to present only those facts that are legally significant or that are necessary to make the problem clear. At the same time, bear in mind that the office memo should be a stand-alone document that can fully inform any colleague in your law office who may read it; therefore, the facts section should always contain a full and coherent recitation of the relevant facts, whether or not the principal reader of the memo already knows them (unless, of course, you were instructed to do otherwise).

4) The overall conclusion contains a summary of the main points of your analysis. In your application section you may have struggled with areas of uncertainty in the legal doctrine and/or competing policy rationales. You may have also grappled with a seemingly contradictory assortment of facts: some seem to fit into the requirements of the rule; others suggest that the rule is not satisfied. You may have weighed arguments against counterarguments. After you have done all this, you must take a position and make a statement about how the court will apply the law. Given the more fully fleshed out short answer, the writer here has opted for a brief restatement of the ultimate conclusion.

Supplementary Readings
拓展阅读

TO: Kelly Anderson, Marketing Executive
FROM: Jonathon Fitzgerald, Market Research Assistant
DATE: June 14, 2007
SUBJECT: Fall Clothes Line Promotion

Market research and analysis show that the proposed advertising media for the new fall lines need to be reprioritized and changed. Findings from focus groups and surveys have made it apparent that we need to update our advertising efforts to align them with the styles and trends of young adults today. No longer are young adults interested in sitcoms as they watch reality televisions shows. Also, it is has become increasingly important to use the internet as a tool to communicate with our target audience to show our dominance in the clothing industry.

Internet Advertising

XYZ Company needs to focus advertising on internet sites that appeal to young people. According to surveys, 72% of our target market uses the internet for five hours or more per week. The following list shows in order of popularity the most frequented sites:

- Google
- Facebook
- Myspace
- EBay
- iTunes

Shifting our efforts from our other media sources such as radio and magazine to these popular internet sites will more effectively promote our product sales. Young adults are spending more and more time on the internet downloading music, communicating and researching for homework and less and less time reading paper magazines and listening to the radio. As the trend for cultural icons to go digital, so must our marketing plans.

Television Advertising

It used to be common to advertise for our products on shows like *Friends* and *Seinfeld* for our target audience, but even the face of television is changing. Young adults are tuning into reality television shows for their entertainment. Results from the focus group show that our target audience is most interested in shows like *American Idol*, *The Apprentice*, and *America's Next Top Model*. The only non-reality television show to be ranked in the top ten most commonly watched shows by males and females 18-25 is *Desperate Housewives*. At Blue Incorporated, we need to focus our advertising budget on reality television shows and reduce the amount of advertising spent on other programs.

By refocusing our advertising efforts of our new line of clothing we will be able to maximize the exposure of our product to our target market and therefore increase our sales. Tapping into the trends of young adults will help us gain market share and sales through effective advertising.

Attachments: Focus Group Results, January- May 2007; Survey Findings, January - April 2007

（文献来源：https://owl. english. purdue. edu/owl/resource/590/04/）

Reading Comprehension

1. What are the main sections that this memo can be divided into?
2. What are the purpose and focus of this memo?
3. Is there any place in this memo that needs to be improved?

Exercise 课后练习

● True or False

Directions: Read the following sentences and decide whether they are true or false.

1. One essential portion of a memo is the task statement.
2. Summary segment is necessary for short memos.
3. Closing segment should be 1/4 of the memo.

● Gap-Filling

Directions: Complete each sentence with appropriate words.

1. The context is _____, _____, or _____ of the problem you are solving.
2. Make sure you document _____ or provide _____ whenever necessary.
3. The format of a memo follows the general guidelines of _____.

● Short Answer Questions

Directions: Answer the following questions briefly.

1. What is the twofold purpose of memos?
2. How to show it is a new paragraph?

● Simulative Exercise

After reading these tips above, try to write a memo.

In order to discuss dormitory security issue, as the monitor of Class 10, you're going to inform your classmates to attend class meeting at 4 p.m., Jan 3rd, 2018.

Business Letters
商务信函

Abstract
内容概览

A business letter is usually a letter from one company to another, or between such organizations and their customers, clients and other external parties. Business letters can have many types of contents, for example to request direct information or action from another party, to order supplies from a supplier, to point out a mistake by the letter's recipient, to reply directly to a request, to apologize for a wrong, or to convey goodwill. A business letter is sometimes useful because it produces a permanent written record, and may be taken more seriously by the recipient than other forms of communication.[1]

商务信函通常指由一家公司给另一家公司的信件，或是这些组织与其客户、委托人和其他外部机构之间的信件。根据内容，商务信函分为很多种，例如在信中要求另一方提供直接信息或行动、从供应商处订购产品、指出收件人所犯的错误、直接回复请求、为错误道歉，或是转达友好意愿。商务信函有时颇为有效，因为它会是永久的书面记录，而且可能会比其他交流形式更容易被收件人认真对待。

---

[1] M.E. Guffey and Dana Loewy. *Business Communication: Process and Product*. Third Brief Canadian Edition. Thomson-Nelson, 2010. pp. 183–214.

商务信函 | Business Letters

Basic Knowledge 基础知识

Introduction

Your business letter is a representation of your company, so you want it to look distinctive and immediately communicate "high quality". Business letter serves as the bridge to communicate with the various parties. The functions of business letters are multidimensional. The importance of business letter is presented below through its various functions or objectives:

Building Goodwill

One of the important purposes of a business letter is to sell the good reputation and friendliness of a company. It acts as an ambassador of a country for the company. It aims at building goodwill in customers-company relationship, holding present customers, reviving inactive accounts and inviting customers to buy more and varied products.

Records and References

Business letter are very useful as records and references of previous transactions. In business, innumerable transactions or communications occur with a large number of people that are not possible for a businessman to remember. When memory fails, business letters act as previous records and can be used for future reference.

Making a Lasting Impression

In case of oral communication, the impact of any message is felt mainly during the time of hearing. And as soon as the next oral communication takes place, the effect of the previous one is reduced. But a letter makes a lasting impression on the readers' mind as it stays with them and works effectively every time it is read.

Building and Maintaining Business Relation

Business letters help to build and maintain business relation among various parties like manufacturers, distributors, intermediaries, support services and consumers.

To Exchange Business Information

The prime objective of a business letter is to exchange business related information between the parties involved. Most of the time business people send letters to their counter-parties containing various business information.

Widening the Approach

It is very difficult to send business representatives to all the places. But a letter can be sent any place at any distance. Sometimes executives, professionals, politicians, etc. are difficult to be approached personally. But a letter can find easy access to anybody. Thus a business letter helps to widen the area of business operations and also the access to a large number of people.

An Authoritative Proof

A business letter also serves the purpose of evidence. A written commitment binds the concerned parties to obey to the text of writing. A letter signed by a responsible person acts as an authoritative proof of what is said in it. It can even be treated as a valid document that can be produced as evidence in a court of law if any dispute arises.

Others

Business letter also has some other functions beside the above ones. It provides legal facility, saves time, helps to increase products, demand, helps to settle transaction easily and it is accepted by all as a reliable media of communication.[①]

简介

商务信函代表着整个公司的形象,因此写信方会希望它与众不同,并立即传达出"高质量"的信息。商务信函是与各方沟通的桥梁,其功能是多维的。接下来我们将通过描述商务信函不同的功能和目的来呈现其重要性。

建立良好信誉

商务信函的一个重要目的是传达公司良好的信誉以及友好态度。它就像是公司的大使,致力于建立顾客与公司间的友好关系,保留住现有客户,给闲置的账户注入活力,并吸引顾客购买更多数量及更多种类的产品。

记录及参考

商务信函可以作为以往交易的记录和参考,因此对公司非常有帮助。无数

---

① [Bizcom Coach, What is Business Letter? Objectives of Business Letter,] https://vpn-2. ucsd. edu/+CSCO+00756767633A2F2F6F766D70627A7A686176706E6776626E170626E70752E70627A++/what-is-business-letter-objectives-of-business-letter/

的交易和沟通发生在商业领域的人群之间,而商人是不可能记住这些的。此时,商务信函可作为以前的记录,并可用于将来的参考。

留下持久印象

在口头交流中,所有信息只在听的那一时刻有影响力,但当下一次口头交流开始时,前一次交流的效果就会降低。但是,信件会给读者留下持久的印象,因为每次只要打开阅读,它就能发挥作用。

建立和维持业务关系

商务信函有助于和各方建立业务和维持关系,如制造商、分销商、中介、辅助性服务者及消费者。

交流商务信息

商务信函的主要目的在于各方之间交换业务信息。大多数时候,商务人士会彼此发送包含各种商业信息的信件。

拓宽交流方式

要把业务代表送到各个地方是非常困难的。但信件可以寄到任何地方。有时,我们很难亲身接触到高管、专业人士、政界人士等,但是,信件可以轻易到达任何人那里。因此,商务信函有助于拓宽业务运营的领域,同时也有助于接触到更多的人。

成为具有权威性的证据

商务信函也能够发挥提供证据的作用。书面承诺促使相关各方遵守文本内容。信件一经担保人签署,其内容就可得到权威性的证明。它甚至可以作为一份有效的文件,在争议发生时,在法庭上作为证据。

其他

除上述内容之外,商务信函还有一些其他的功能,如提供法律帮助、节省时间、增加产品、提出需求,有助于交易便利化,它可被所有人接受为可靠的沟通媒介。

Writing Requirement

Parts of a Business Letter

Sender's Address

The sender's address usually is included in letterhead. If you are not using letterhead, include the sender's address at the top of the letter one line above the date. Do not write the sender's name or title, as it is included in the letter's closing. Include only the street address, city, and zip code.

Date

The date line is used to indicate the date the letter was written. However, if your letter is completed over a number of days, use the date it was finished in the date line. When writing to companies within the United States, use the American date format. (The United States-based convention for formatting a date places the month before the day. For example: June 11, 2001.) Write out the month, day and year two inches from the top of the page.

Inside Address

The inside address is the recipient's address. It is always best to write to a specific individual at the firm to which you are writing. If you do not have the person's name, do some research by calling the company or speaking with employees from the company. Include a personal title such as Ms. , Mrs. , Mr. , or Dr. Follow a woman's preference in being addressed as Miss, Mrs. , or Ms. If you are unsure of a woman's preference in being addressed, use Ms. If there is a possibility that the person to whom you are writing is a Dr. or has some other title, use that title. Usually, people will not mind being addressed by a higher title than they actually possess. To write the address, use the U. S. Post Office Format. For international addresses, type the name of the country in all-capital letters on the last line. The inside address begins one line below the date. It should be left justified, no matter which format you are using.

Salutation

Use the same name as the inside address, including the personal title. If you know the person and typically address them by their first name, it is acceptable to use only the first name in the salutation (for example: Dear Lucy:). In all other cases, however, use the personal title and last/family name followed by a colon. Leave one line blank after the salutation.

If you don't know a reader's gender, use a nonsexist salutation, such as their job title followed by the receiver's name. It is also acceptable to use the full name in a salutation if you cannot determine gender. For example, you might write Dear Chris Harmon: if you were unsure of Chris's gender.

Body

For block and modified block formats, single space and left justify each paragraph within the body of the letter. Leave a blank line between each paragraph.

When writing a business letter, be careful to remember that conciseness is very important. In the first paragraph, consider a friendly opening and then a statement of the main point. The next paragraph should begin justifying the importance of the main point. In the next few paragraphs, continue justification with background information and supporting details. The closing paragraph should restate the purpose of the letter and, in some cases, request some type of action.

Closing

The closing begins at the same vertical point as your date and one line after the last body paragraph. Capitalize the first word only (for example: Thank you) and leave four lines between the closing and the sender's name for a signature. If a colon follows the salutation, a comma should follow the closing; otherwise, there is no punctuation after the closing.

Enclosures

If you have enclosed any documents along with the letter, such as a resume, you indicate this simply by typing Enclosures one line below the closing. As an option, you may list the name of each document you are including in the envelope. For instance, if you have included many documents and need to ensure that the recipient is aware of each document, it may be a good idea to list the names.

Typist Initials

Typist initials are used to indicate the person who typed the letter. If you typed the letter yourself, omit the typist initials.[①]

写作要求

商务信函的组成

寄件人地址

寄件人的地址通常写在信纸抬头。如果你不写在信头，请在日期上方一行的位置写上发件人的地址。不要写寄件人的姓名或头衔，因为它包含在信件的结尾。只用写清楚街道地址、城市和邮政编码。

日期

日期行用来表示写信的日期。但是，如果你的信件是用了多天才完成的，那就将完成的那一天写在日期行上。在给美国的公司写信时，要使用美国的日

---

① https://owl.english.purdue.edu/owl/resource/653/1/

期格式（美国的日期格式规定将月份写在日期之前，如：June 11, 2001）把月、日和年写在离页面顶部2英寸的地方。

信内地址

信内地址即信内收件人地址。当你寄信给一个公司时，你最好写给一个属于该公司的个人。如果你不清楚这个人的名字，可以打电话给公司或是公司的员工进行询问。写上如女士、太太、先生或是博士等个人头衔。对于女性，你可以称她为小姐、太太或女士。如果你不确定该如何称呼，可以称她为女士。如果你要写给博士或是拥有其他头衔的人，就直接用头衔进行称呼。人们往往不介意被更高的头衔所称呼。请记得用美国邮局格式来写地址。国际地址要在最后一行输入国家名称的大写字母。信内地址写在日期的下一行。无论哪一种格式，这一部分都应设置为左对齐。

称呼

在这一部分，要写上信内地址中收件人的名字，包括他/她的头衔。如果你认识这个人，并且通常用他们的名字称呼他们，那么在称呼这一部分中直呼其名是可以接受的（例如：Dear Lucy:）除此之外，都需要写上头衔、姓氏及冒号。在问候这一部分之后要空出一行。

如果你不知道收件人的性别，那就用一种非性别歧视的称呼，如工作职位加上收件人姓名。在这种情况下，也可以称呼其全名。比如说，你不确定克里斯的性别，就可以写"亲爱的克里斯·哈蒙"。

主体

对于齐头式及修正齐头式（混合式）格式来说，使用单倍行距，每段均左对齐，段落与段落之间需空一行。在写商务信函时，要记住非常重要的一点是简明。第一段应以友善的语言作开场白，之后，陈述要点。第二段应着手证明要点的重要性。在接下来的几段中，继续以背景信息和有支撑作用的细节来证明要点的合理性。结尾段应重审这封信的目的或是要求做出某种行动。

结束语

结束语与日期垂直对齐，并位于主题段落的一行之后的位置。在这一部分，只用将第一个单词的首字母大写（例如：Thank you）并与寄件人的签字之间空4行。如果问候部分以冒号结束，那么结束语部分应以逗号结束，相反，如果问候部分没有标点符号来结尾的话，结束语后面也不用加标点符号。

附件

如果你随信附上了任何文件，如简历，你只用在结束语下一行打上"附件"的字样就可以起到告知对方的作用。另外，你可以列出所有信中所包含文件的名称。比如，你已经附上了很多文件并且需要确保收件人知道每个文件，那么你最好列出它们的名称。

打字员姓名首字母缩写

将打字员名字的首字母缩写可以表明谁是打字者。如果是作者自己打了这封信，就可以省略这一部分。

Case Studies 案例分析

I. Invitation Letter

(print business Letters of Invitation on corporate letterhead)

August 15, 20xx

Mr. Roger Moriarity
Executive Director
Children With Disabilities Foundation
430 Smithson Drive, Suite 500
Chicago, IL 32956

Dear Mr. Moriarity:

The purpose of this letter is to formally invite you, on behalf of the Board of Directors, to be the Closing Keynote Speaker at the upcoming 20xx International Disabled Children Research Institute (IDCRI) Conference.

The theme of this conference is "Disabling the Disability — Looking It Straight In the Eye". It will be held at the Mountainview Conference Facility, in Montpelier, Vermont from December 3 to 5, 20xx.

For you information, Susan Crutchlow of Taming the Environment will be the opening Keynote Speaker. The provisional title of her presentation is "The Disabled Environment — Can We Help It?" We will forward a complete draft speaker program to you in a couple of weeks to give you an idea of the specific subjects that will be covered by the other speakers.

We expect attendance this year to be the highest ever; in the area of 2000 delegates and 150 speakers. This includes a large contingent from our new European Chapter that is based in Geneva. You may have heard that Dr. Walton Everinson will be presenting a major paper on his latest research into "Genetic ReEngineering". We are already receiving inquiries from all over the world about Dr. Everinson's presentation.

In closing, we would be pleased and honored if you would consent to be our closing speaker at the 20xx IDCRI Conference.

I will call you in a week or so to follow up on this.

Yours sincerely,

Richard Bagnall
Executive Director

（文献来源：http://www. writinghelp-central. com/invitation-letter. html. ）

Analysis

Invitation letters can be written for a wide variety of business and personal situations. The sample letter above typical of one that would be used in a business or academic environment. They should be short and to the point, ideally ending with a statement about how the invitation will be followed up.

II. Business Thank You Letter

(print Business Thank You Letter on corporate letterhead paper)

March 15, 20xx

Mr. Alphonse Germanian
President and CEO
BioDynamics Llc.
1525 Broadway, Suite 4500
New York, NY 10034

Dear Mr. Germanian:

As Chairperson of the Corporate Conscience Campaign — Helping the Homeless in New York, I am writing this to thank you personally for your company's support in last month's fund-raising effort.

As I indicated when we spoke on the phone two weeks ago, the campaign was considered a resounding success, raising a total of $1. 65 million to-date, significantly exceeding our target of $1 million. Some donations are still trickling in, so we could end up close to a total of $2 million.

BioDynamics was an influential leader throughout the entire three-month campaign. In fact, we couldn't have succeeded without the generous support of your company, both financially, and through your organizational and administrative assistance. Your Team Leader, Kathryn Gomez was particularly impressive, going above and beyond what we could have expected of someone performing as a volunteer while continuing on with her day-to-day duties. Please convey my special thanks to Kathryn.

I would also ask you to convey my sincere thanks and congratulations to all of those other people in your company who contributed in any way to the Helping the Homeless Campaign. Please tell them that the sum of their contributions resulted in a major success that they should all be proud of taking part in.

I believe that the 27 companies that participated in this effort have set a new standard for social responsibility in this community, and have set a powerful example that will inspire other companies and organizations to do the same.

I look forward to seeing you at the Mayor's special thank you reception next month.

Yours sincerely,

Jackson Pritchard
Fundraising Chair

（文献来源：http://www.writinghelp-central.com/business-thankyou-letter.html.）

Analysis

Well written thank you letters are important in many different business situations. The real-life business thank you letter is a typical example of such a letter. It's a timely letter, written for an appropriate business situation.

III. Apology Letter

(print business Apology Letter on corporate letterhead paper)

June 28, 20xx
Ms. Rebecca Winston

2595 Dewdrop Circle
Unit No. 29
Birmingham, AL 35233

Dear Ms. Winston:

The purpose of this is to convey to you my sincere apologies for any inconvenience you may have experienced last month with respect to the installation of your Internet high speed service.

I just returned from vacation this week and found your file in my in-basket. As soon as I reviewed your case it was clear that somehow your May 20th request for a change in service had somehow slipped through the cracks. The only possible explanation I can give is that we have recently had a number of key staff changes which might have resulted in your letter being overlooked.

Consequently, I have directed our Installation Group to contact you by the end of this week to set up a time convenient to you when they could go to your house and install your new router and make the necessary adjustments to your software.

Because of this serious oversight, and as a testament to our appreciation of you as our customer, we are going to provide you with your first three months of high speed service free of charge. Therefore, your account will not be billed until October of this year.

Ms. Quinlan, let me assure you that what happened in your case is not typical of CableNet's level of customer service. We continue to be committed to providing you and all of our customers with the highest standards of service in the industry.

If you have any questions please don't hesitate to call me at 205-754-9785.

Yours in service,

Paul Cordero
Manager, Customer Solutions

（文献来源：http://www. writinghelp-central. com/apology-letter. html. ）

Analysis

This sample apology letter was sent from a company to a customer to deal with a case of very poor customer service. These letters must be sincere, or there is no point. It's unfortunate that more companies don't send such letters of apology to poorly served customers.

Supplementary Readings
拓展阅读

(print this letter on business letterhead paper)

January 20, 20xx

Mrs. Belinda Huffman
1541 Aberdeen Ave.
Montreal, QC
H3C 1L2

Dear Mrs. Huffman:
Re: Private Preview Showing — Spring Collection 20xx — Ticket No. 12-0127

As one of our longtime valued customers we would like to invite you to our special Private Preview Showing of our Spring Fashion Collection for 20xx.

The showing will take place at our downtown store at 4550 Sherbrooke St. West, Monday evening, February 19, 20xx from 7:00 p.m to 11:00 p.m. Limited free parking will be available in our parking garage on the Mountain Street side of the store.

In addition to the continuous fashion show that will be running all evening long, there will be a number of spring merchandise draws, as well as a door prize for a $2,000 unlimited shopping spree. So, don't miss out on the fun!

For entry into the show and to be eligible for any of the draws you will be required to produce this original invitation with your ticket number printed on it.

In order that we may plan for snacks and refreshments appropriately, if you plan to attend, we ask you to please call Danielle Laporte at (514) 982-7593 and advise her by February 12th.

Please note: If Danielle doesn't hear from you by Friday, February 10th we will assume that you are not attending the show and we will issue your ticket number to someone else.

Everyone here at The Fashion House looks forward to meeting you and sharing our Spring Collection with you at our Preview Private Showing.

Yours sincerely,

Rhonda Sugarman
Show Co-ordinator

（文献来源：http://www.writinghelp-central.com/letter-of-invitation.html.）

Reading Comprehension

1. What is the type of this business letter?
2. What are the features of this business letter?
3. Is there any room for improving this business letter?

Exercise 课后练习

● **True or False**

Directions: Read the following sentences and decide whether they are true or false.

1. The overall style of letter depends on the relationship between the parties concerned.
2. The functions of business letters are unidimensional, for communication.
3. A business letter can serve as a proof, but can not be produced as evidence in a court of law.

● **Gap-Filling**

Directions: Complete each sentence with appropriate words.

1. The prime objective of a business letter is to _____ between the parties involved. Most of the time business people send letters to their counter-parties containing various business information.
2. A Business Letter contains _____ parts; they are _____.

● **Short Answer Questions**

Directions: Answer the following questions briefly.

1. What is the functions of a business letter?
2. Can you name several kinds of business letters?

● **Simulative Exercise**

After learning the functions and Writing Requirements of business letter, try to write a business letter in which you need to order supplies from a supplier.

10 Chapter

Business Report
商业报告

Abstract
内容概览

Organizations need accurate, timely, objective and concise information to make effective decisions. One way they can obtain such information is from a business report. This document can be defined as "an organized presentation of information to a specific audience for the purpose of helping an organization achieve an objective".[1]

Writing an effective business report is a necessary skill for communicating ideas in the business environment. Reports usually address a specific issue or problem, and are often commissioned when a decision needs to be made. They present the author's findings in relation to the issue or problem and then recommend a course of action for the organization to take. The key to a good report is in-depth analysis. Good writers will show their reader how they have interpreted their findings. The reader will understand the basis on which the conclusions are drawn as well as the rationale for the recommendations.

企业需要准确、及时、客观和简明的信息来做出有效决策。商业报告是企业获取这些信息的有效途径。此类文件可被定义为"为了帮助企业实现目标而向特定受众群体提供有条理的信息"。

撰写有效的商业报告是在商业环境中交流想法的必备技能。商业报告通常涉及具体事件或问题，经常需要在做出决定前完成。商业报告表明了作者对于问题的发现，然后向企业提出行动方针供其采纳。写出一篇优秀报告的关键是

---

[1] J. P. Bowman, and B. P. Branchaw, *Business Report Writing*, 2nd ed, Chicago: The Dryden Press, 1988, p. 12.

深入分析。优秀的撰写者会向读者展示他们如何解读自己的发现。读者将理解得出结论的依据和提出建议的理由。

Basic Knowledge 基础知识

Introduction

Business reports can take different forms. Generally, they are concise documents that first inform by summarizing and analyzing key facts and situations and then make recommendations to the person or group asking for the report.

Essay and business report need to include standard formal English. However, there are some key differences between the two genres:①

	Essay	Business Report
Purpose	Articulate a point of view in relation to a particular proposition	Often recommend action to solve a specific problem
Format & Structure	Have introduction, body and conclusion sections that normally do not use headings	Always have sections clearly divided by numbered headings (and often sub-headings)
	Use cohesive paragraphs to link ideas rather than list dot-points	Use shorter, more concise paragraphs and dot-points where applicable
Abstract	Typically don't normally need an abstract as readers read the text carefully from start to finish	Always have an abstract (or executive summary) as readers are typically "time poor" and skim and scan through the text quickly
Graphics	Rarely use graphics as written evidence	Feature graphics (such as tables and graphs) for supporting main points
Writer	Are generally the result of individual work	Are often the result of group work

---

① M. Eggins, Business report helpsheet, the University of Melbourne, http://www. library. unimelb. edu. au/libraries/bee.

（续表）

| Reader | Are written for the lecturer/tutor or other academic audiences | Are addressed to a specific audience (i.e., client or manager) established by the topic |

简介

商业报告可以采取不同的形式。一般来说，商业报告属于简明扼要的文件。首先总结和分析关键事实和情况，然后向需要得到报告的个人或团体提出建议。

论文和商业报告需要使用标准正式英语。但是，两种写作类型也存在着一些重要差异：

	论文	商业报告
目的	阐明与特定命题有关的观点	经常建议采取行动来解决具体问题
格式与结构	有引言、正文和结论部分，通常不使用标题	经常使用带数字的标题（也包括副标题）将各部分分得很清楚
	使用连贯的段落连接想法，而不是列出项目符号	在合适的地方使用更短、更简洁的段落和项目符号
摘要	因为读者要从头到尾仔细阅读报告，通常不需要摘要	总含有摘要（或执行摘要），因为读者通常没有时间仔细阅读全文，只能略读和浏览文本
图表	很少将图形作为书面例子	有特征图形（如表格和图形），用于支撑要点
作者	通常是个人独立完成	通常是团队协作完成
读者	是为讲师/导师或其他专业人士撰写的	针对相关主题下的特定受众（如客户或经理）

Writing Requirement

A business report should contain the following parts:

1. Title Page: title of your report, your name, student number and your course.
2. Table of Contents: headings, subheadings and page numbers

3. Executive summary: summarizes your whole report, and gives your reader a clear idea of what your report says, without needing to read it. Start with the report's purpose, then give your scope, main points, and a summary of your findings and recommendations.

4. Introduction: summarizes the issue or problem, its background and context, why it matters, why you're looking into it and the scope of the task. You can also introduce your approach and explain your methodology in finding and sorting data.

5. Literature Review: some reports require extra readings on the topic. This is where you research peer-reviewed articles about the problem to let your client know what the literature says.

6. Method: explain how you did the research. Did you interview teenagers on consumer behavior? Did you give a survey out to 50 teenagers, and based your report on these results? Did you investigate the market trends affecting teenagers in the past 20 years? In this section you should show numbers, graphs, charts and tables with your data. This section may include:

- the type of research design, e.g.qualitative or quantitative?
- sampling procedure, e.g.did you use probability sampling or non-probability sampling techniques and why?
- data collection procedure, e.g.how was the data/information collected? Did you do face-to-face interviews? What are the sources of your information and why did you choose them?
- data analysis procedure, e.g.how was the data/information analysed and why?

7. Findings: this will make up the bulk of your report. This section lists your key findings when you applied your methodology and conducted your research.

8. Discussions: explain the facts you discovered in your "Findings" section and tell us what they mean. What implications do they have? What conclusions do you have about them? Once you answer these questions, it will be easy for you to plan the solutions.

9. Recommendations: explains the strategies you suggest to deal with the conclusion from your findings, or to solve the original problem. Indicate the benefits of each solution, e.g. return on investment or increase in sales. Recommendations are not your personal opinion. Your findings, your research and your data are the reasons (or evidence) behind your recommendations.

商业报告 | Business Report

10. Conclusion: wrap it all up and tell us what will happen next. Where should your client go from here? What's the next step for them?

11. References: a list of sources you cited in your report, such as a book with data you used, or an article from an expert you quoted. As long as you read a piece of information somewhere and used it in your report, you should include it in the References section.

12. Appendices: detailed charts, survey examples, transcripts, or related reports.[①]

写作要求

一篇商业报告应该含有以下几个方面：

1. 标题页：报告题目、作者姓名、学号及课程名称。

2. 目录：包括标题、子标题以及页码。

3. 执行摘要：总结整个报告，让你的读者不需要读整篇报告就能清楚地知道你的报告内容。首先，阐明报告的目的。然后，给出你的范围、主要观点以及对你的发现和建议的总结。

4. 简介：总结事件或问题，包括它的背景、为什么它很重要、为什么你要调查它以及任务的范围。你也可以介绍你的研究方法，还可以阐明你在寻找和搜集资料时用的方法。

5. 文献综述：有些报告需要额外的文献阅读。在这一部分，你会去研究有关同一问题的同行评议过的论文。这样一来，你的客户才会清楚文中内容是什么。

6. 方法：解释你是如何做研究的。你采访过青少年消费者的行为吗？你是否对50名青少年进行过调查，并根据调查结果来撰写你的报告？你是否调查了过去20年中影响青少年的市场趋势？在这一部分，你应该使用有关数据的各类数字、图形、图表和表格。这一部分应包括：

● 研究设计的类型，如，是定性的还是定量的？

● 抽样过程，如，你使用了概率抽样还是非概率抽样技术，为什么？

● 数据收集过程，如，数据/信息是如何收集起来的？你做了面对面的采访吗？你的信息来源是什么？为什么选择它们？

● 数据分析程序，如，你是如何分析数据/信息的，为什么？

---

① Writing a Business Report: Writing Centre Learning Guide, The University of Adelaide, https://www.adelaide.edu.au/.../learningGuide_BusinessReportWriting.pdf

7. 结果/结论：这将是你报告的重点。当你应用你的方法并进行研究时，你要在这一部分列出主要发现。

8. 讨论：解释你在"调查结果"部分中发现的事实，并告诉读者它们的意思。它们意味着什么？通过它们能得出什么结论？一旦你回答了这些问题，规划出解决方案就会更加容易。

9. 建议：阐释你建议使用的方法策略，主要用于如何从调查结果中得出结论或是如何解决最初的问题。指出每个解决方案的收益，如投资回报或销售增加。这一部分不应该是你的个人观点。你的建议应建立在调查发现、调查本身以及数据/证据的基础上。

10. 总结：总结你的报告，然后告诉我们对未来的预测。你的客户下一步何去何从？有什么具体打算？

11. 参考文献：列出你在报告中引用的文献来源，例如，你使用过其数据的书籍，你引用过的某一位专业人士写的文章。只要你在某处读了有关信息并在报告中用到了它，你就需要在参考文献这一部分将它列出来。

12. 附录：列出详细图表、调查案例、文本或相关报告。

Case Studies
案例分析

Report on Central Purchasing Policy

April 2015

Matthew Nash

Summary

This report into the central purchasing policy of Smith and Co. will assess how the policy currently works and it will address concerns about the recent decline in regional sales.

Introduction

This report addresses branch managers' concerns with the central purchasing policy. These concerns arose from a steady decline in regional sales. It has been suggested that we should reintroduce the previous purchasing system to prevent a further drop in sales: this report will assess the current situation and make recommendations for what action could be taken.

Method

Interviews were carried out with each of our 20 branch managers within the last month. They were questioned about their objections to the central policy and asked to identify its main failings.

Research into our main competitors' practices and sales was also undertaken by personal visits to stores and assessment of sales figures in the trade press.

Findings

1. Existing Situation

The central purchasing policy was implemented in January 2005. It replaced the previous system where regional managers were responsible for purchasing and could select lines likely to appeal to customers in their area. Since the central purchasing policy was implemented there has been a steady reduction in regional sales (see Appendix A) and a subsequent demand from our branches to return to the previous system.

However, the central purchasing policy has proved to be efficient and cost-effective over the past year, especially in terms of reducing storage overheads (see Appendix B.)

2. Branch Managers' Concerns

Interviews with managers indicated that dissatisfaction with the existing policy reached a peak after the Christmas 2006 sales period, when regional sales were significantly lower year-on-year as managers had predicted.

In every shop, managers highlighted lines that were previously stocked because they had a specific appeal for customers in their area but which had not been ordered by central purchasing this year because they were unlikely to do well across the country as a whole. Managers also reported that many customers had requested such lines, especially over the Christmas period. Conversely, there were many examples of stock received by branches which were of no interest to customers in their area and which subsequently remained unsold.

3. Competitors' Practice

Visits to competitors' stores revealed that they all held stock with a regional appeal. A review of sales figures for these lines in the Monthly Trade Journal during the period July 2005 to January 2007 shows that we have missed out on a sizeable amount of revenue by not stocking such items. (Statistics are attached in Appendix C.)

Conclusions

While savings have been made, the existing situation is unsatisfactory and could seriously damage the company's market share if allowed to continue. Action should be taken to address managers' concerns and prevent a further decline in sales. There are three possible courses of action:

1. to continue with the central purchasing policy
2. to modify this system to address its drawbacks
3. to return to the former system of regional buying

Recommendations

1. Given that the central purchasing policy, although cost-effective, has resulted in a decline in sales, it would appear that continuing with this system without modification is not advisable.

2. Consideration should be given to allocating a small proportion of the annual budget to regional managers to allow them to buy in lines with known local appeal. This could be trialed and sales could be monitored for a fixed period, after which time the situation could be reviewed again if necessary.

3. A return to the previous system of regional buying would seem undesirable, given that the central purchasing policy is both efficient and cost-effective.

（文献来源：https://oup. useremarkable. com/production/images/uploads/3676/original/sample_Business_Report. pdf?1479137052. ）

Analysis

This business report focuses on central purchasing policy and aims at evaluating how the present policy works and addressing concerns about the recent decline in regional sales. To achieve this objective, the report carries out interviews and personal visits to get a better understanding of themselves as well as their major competitors. According to what they've found, the report details the existing situation, branch managers' concerns and competitors' practice. The rest of the report further points out conclusions and recommendations for policy-makers to take reference from.

Supplementary Readings
拓展阅读

Report on Eco-Homes Project

1. Title of Business Report
Title: Eco-Homes Project Initiative
Objective: Compile data and analysis for development for housing project Eco-Homes at location and address of the project.
Report by: Dr. Larry Marshall, CEO EcoVision Projects, Empire Construction and Infrastructure Group.
Key Contents: A Detailed plan, proposition, execution schedule and analysis of the project idea of an eco-friendly settlement put forth by Dr. Jason Smith, New Projects Department, Empire Construction and Infrastructure Group (mother company).
Reporting and Analysis Time: 1 month
Project Implementation Time: 17 months
Assumptions: The time frame and execution is framed, taking into consideration the seasonal elements of climate and other turnover ratios, experienced in the previous financial year.

2. Letter of Transmittal
Attached, letter of transmittal, conveying the idea by Dr Smith, consisting of the core features of report.

3. Table of Contents
Summary and Synopsis of the Project

Introduction

Discussion and Details

Conclusion

Recommendations

4. Summary and Synopsis

The Eco-Homes Project Initiative is an underway project which has been conceived by the Empire Group. The basic ideology of the initiative is eco-friendly living. The Empire group intends to build a mega residential complex which is spread over 35 acres of land, and house around about 150 households, which are self-sufficient in several ways. The complex thrives on the basis of inbuilt agricultural center, animal husbandry center, building gardens, fuel cell and bio-gas-propane generators of electricity, massive solar panels which provide heat to the homes and also electricity. The complex will span over the 35 acre premise and will consist of 3 core residential centers, 15 solar panel driven green houses, 2 orchards, 5 gardens, 3 pastures and 3 animal husbandry centers cum dairies and a staff of 33 people.

5. Discussion and Details

Some common points, details and conclusions that were drawn in the meeting of project engineers, company architects, cost accountants and the CFA's go as follows.

The project will bring a substantial revenue if all 150 houses are sold off at a price of amount per house hold. The project will be a highly big commercial success as it is not just situated in the city but, once the customer buys the housing facility his usual bills that include, electricity and water bill will be cut down to half. The only con that is foreseen is that the sale value is huge.

There are 5 phases of the project, namely, the basic foundation phase, housing complex 1 phase, followed by 2 and 3, with the last phase being the development of all the support and infrastructure facility. It is estimated that every phase would go on for 3 months plus a backup of 2 months has been provided.

商业报告 | Business Report

The sales for real estate would begin with the completion of housing complex 1, followed by complex 2 and 3. By the end of complex 3, the real estate market rates would have increased by 7.8%. This price escalation however is not included in any of the calculations.

The cost sheets showing cost projections for the project have been attached.

A 5 year maintenance, free of cost has been provided for the complex. An operation cost of about $500 per 2 months is to be paid by every household to keep the operations going.

6. Conclusion

The project team recommends that this project should be taken up and executed as fast as possible as the real estate market is and the eco-friendly products have been consistently showing positive rises in the past 5 years.

7. Recommendation

In order to reduce operational cost of $500 for every two months, which is incurred by the residents, the project team recommends more research and development. It a selling point that can be put forth to boost sales.

(文献来源：www.buzzle.com/articles/business-report-example.html.)

Reading Comprehension

1. What is the report about?
2. What is the basic ideology of the Eco-Homes Project Initiative?
3. What are the differences between this report and the one in Case studies?

Exercise 课后练习

● **True or False**

Directions: Read the following sentences and decide whether they are true or false.

1. The key to a good report is in-depth analysis.
2. Academic writing and business report share no difference between their genres.
3. You only need to list the article from which you quoted in the References section.

● **Gap–Filling**

Directions: Complete each sentence with appropriate words.

1. In the Introduction section, you should summarize the issue or problem, its _____ and _____. You can also introduce your _____ and explain your _____ in finding and sorting data.
2. In _____ section, you research _____ articles about the problem to let your client know what the _____ says.

● **Short Answer Questions**

Directions: Answer the following questions briefly.

1. What is the key to a good business report?
2. What are the basic parts of a business report?

● **Simulative Exercise**

Based on your understanding of the purpose and requirements of a business report, try to write a report on e-commerce or something else you are interested in.

Part Three　Leisure Writing

第三部分　休闲写作

Chapter 11

Leisure Writing Style
休闲写作概述

Abstract
内容概览

  Writing in a leisurely way makes writing easier. It comes to you naturally. The only struggle you may have is one of knowing what to say first, then second as your thoughts come flooding in. That's where you may need help to formulate the flow and structure so that you stay focused and not sound confused to your reader. However, without help, don't let this deter you. Just keep writing and the thoughts can be structured later.

  Your best bet to sustained writing is one from a deep part of your soul, where the full meaning of each word and experience you share resonates with you and keeps you up at nights. You wouldn't want to go out and if you do, you want to hurry back to not miss a thought or you take a recording device or tablet with you everywhere you go to jot your thoughts down or continue writing.[①]

  休闲写作是一种较为轻松的写作，是你自然流露的感受。因为头脑中思绪繁杂，写作时唯一的难点在于不知道先说什么，后说什么。在设计文章发展及结构这一点上你可能需要一些帮助，以便能够专注于主题，同时也不会使读者感到困惑。但如果没有得到帮助，也不要让这一点妨碍你写作。你只需要继续写下去，之后再调整结构。

  持续写作的最好办法就是从灵魂深处出发，你写的每个词、每一种经历都能在你的内心深处产生共鸣，也能牵挂着你，使你夜不能寐，甚至不愿出门。就算出了门，你也会想要立即赶回来，以防错过了某一个想法。你可以随身携

[①] Corine La Font, What's Your Motivation To Start Writing? The Gleaner, https://jamaicagleaner.com/article/art-leisure/20170115/whats-your-motivation-start-writing

带记录设备或平板电脑，随时随地记下你的想法或继续写作。

The Purposes of Leisure Writing
休闲写作目的

Leisure writing especially targets those who often have difficulty in focusing idea muscles. The nice thing about leisure writing is that it really is like a muscle; the more you use it, the stronger it gets. And just like any other muscle, once it's whipped into shape, it's good for more than just the activity you used to work it out. Doing barbell curls strengthens your biceps. Once strengthened, those bigger arms are good for not just lifting weights, but for lifting, throwing and carrying all kinds of things—whether it be for sports or work or whatever. Similarly, a sufficiently exercised writing muscle is good for generating all kinds of ideas—not just the type you used to work out with. So whether you're a painter, sculptor, photographer, inventor, entrepreneur, or even a writer—leisure writing can help you help yourself to new ideas.[①]

What's more, leisure writing can be particularly helpful tools for accurately capturing positive events. In his book, *Thinking, Fast and Slow*, the psychologist Daniel Kahneman distinguishes between experience and memory, noting that human memory of an experience can easily be altered. With the help of leisure writing, you will reduce the chance that some later event will transform your memory of the day's experiences. So when you feel you have accomplished something, write it down soon, before a client or critic has the opportunity to say something that diminishes that sense of progress.[②]

休闲写作主要针对经常难以集中思想的人群。休闲写作的优点在于它真的就像肌肉：你用得越多，它就会越强壮。就像其他肌肉一样，它一旦被塑好了形，就可以用来从事除锻炼以外的其他活动。做杠铃弯举能够增强你的肱二头肌。一旦肱二头肌被增强，两只强壮的手臂不仅仅能够举重，还可以投掷以及搬运各类物件——无论运动、工作或是其他活动。同样的道理，经过充分锻炼的"写作肌肉"能够产生各种各样的想法——并不仅仅是你经常遇到的那种类

[①] Chris Grundemann, Creative Writing for Fun and Profit, https://chrisgrundemann. com/index. php/2012/creative-writing-fun-profit/

[②] Daniel Kahneman, *Thinking, Fast and Slow*. Macmillan, 2011.

休闲写作概述 | Leisure Writing Style

型。因此，无论你是画家、雕刻家、摄影师、发明家、企业家，还是作家，休闲写作都能够帮助你产生新想法。

更重要的是，休闲写作对于准确捕捉正面事件来说是非常有用的工具。心理学家丹尼尔·卡内曼在他的书《思考，快与慢》(*Thinking, Fast and Slow*) 中，区分了经历与记忆。他指出，人类对经历的记忆很容易被改变。在休闲写作的帮助下，就算日后发生新的事件，也难以改变你对当天经历的记忆。因此，当你觉得自己已经完成了某件事时，在客户或评论家有机会说出一些让你感到沮丧的言辞之前，快把它写下来吧。

The Requirements of Leisure Writing
休闲写作要求

To help you work through writer's block, consider the strategies below.

1. Lose the "I'm just not a writer" syndrome

Everyone has the potential to be a writer. Continuing to tell yourself otherwise is nothing more than an empty excuse. Reverse the energy. You can be a writer. Tell yourself, "I am absolutely capable of writing".

2. Don't wait for perfect words

If every sentence has to be a flawless work of art, then you will sit in fear. The sweat might pour, but the words won't come. Just start writing words on the page. Know that once you have started, you can go back and revise what you have. But until you start, you will never know where you are trying to go. If you are writing on a tight deadline, it is even more critical that you let go of the notion of immediate perfection. One writer friend of mine offered the analogy that writing is like cleaning a messy room: the only way a large mess gets cleaned up is to start tidying one small corner at a time.

3. Talk to yourself — out loud

It's less stressful for most people to chat with a friend over a beer than to write a grant proposal (even if the content of the conversation is the grant proposal in question). In conversation, it's generally accepted that we might have to stop, correct ourselves and continue speaking. Allow yourself that same freedom in your writing process. If that's hard to do, talk out loud to yourself to get the thoughts flowing.

4. Move words, sentences, paragraphs around the page like pieces of a puzzle

The beauty of writing on a computer is that you can move words and groups of words effortlessly. Just reminding yourself of that tends to make it easier to find your writing flow. For those overwhelmed by the amount of ideas banging around in their head, jot the ideas down, one by one, in a loose cross between thought-notes and an organizational outline. Then, you can slowly work your way down your list, flushing out concepts into sentences and paragraphs without worrying that you might forget something critical.

5. Crystallize your point into a few words

When you sit down to write a business pitch, a grant proposal or a speech, be sure that you have done your research and know precisely what you mean to communicate. If you're struggling to write, it may be a sign that you are confused about what you want to say. Condense the main nugget of what you are trying to say into just a short phrase or sentence and you'll have a better shot at composing a tight, organized piece.[①]

为了能够突破写作的瓶颈，请仔细阅读下列方法。

1. 摆脱"我不是作家"综合征

每个人都有当作家的潜力。你要不停地告诉自己，否定自己只不过是空洞的借口。相反，告诉自己，"我绝对有能力写作"。

2. 不要等待完美的词句

如果每句话都必须是一件完美无瑕的艺术品，那么你就会陷入恐慌之中。即使汗如雨下，词句也不会油然而生。所以，直接开始写吧。你要知道，一旦

---

① Catherine Clifford, 8 Writing Strategies for People Who Say They Can't Write, Entrepreneur, https://www.entrepreneur.com/article/233264

休闲写作概述 | Leisure Writing Style

开始写了,你仍可以回看并修改已写的内容。但如果不迈出第一步,你永远不知道会写到哪里。如果你在紧迫的时间内写作,那么更有必要放弃追求完美的想法。我的一个作家朋友将写作比喻为打扫一个凌乱的房间:唯一一个能将一团糟的房间清理干净的方式是每次只清理一个角落。

3. 大声与自己对话

对于大多数人来说,与朋友闲聊的压力远小于写一份拨款申请,即使闲聊的内容与拨款申请有关。众所周知,在谈话中我们可以在需要的时候停下来,纠正自己犯的错误,然后再继续说话。请让自己在写作过程中拥有同样的自由。如果很难做到,那就大声地对自己说话,激活头脑。

4. 像移动拼图版一样在纸上移动字词句段

在电脑上写作的优势在于,你可以毫不费力地移动字词及段落。要提醒自己这样做会让你更容易适应写作流程。对于那些被头脑中大量的想法所淹没的人来说,他们可以把这些想法一个接一个地记下来,在不同想法与结构框架之间做大致的连接。然后,你可以按照你的列表将概念发展成句子和段落,而不必担心会忘记一些关键点。

5. 将观点具体化到几个词

当你坐下来写商业报告、拨款申请或是演讲时,要确保你已经做了足够的研究并且清楚地知道你想要表述什么。如果写作期间碰到了困难,可能意味着你对自己想要说什么仍感到困惑。将你想要说的要点浓缩成一个简短的短语或句子,这样你就很可能创作出一篇紧凑且有条理的文章。

● **True or False**

Directions: Read the following sentences and decide whether they are true or false.

1. The thoughts should be structured first.
2. Leisure writing can be particularly helpful tools for accurately capturing positive events.

3. The words and sentences you write down should be as perfect as possible.

● **Gap–Filling**

Directions: Complete each sentence with appropriate words.

1. A sufficiently exercised writing muscle is good for _____ all kinds of _____ —not just the type you used to work out with.
2. If you're struggling to write, it may be a sign that you are _____ about what you want to say. _____ the main nugget of what you are trying to say into just a short phrase or sentence and you'll have a better shot at composing a tight, _____ piece

● **Short Answer Questions**

Directions: Answer the following questions briefly.

1. Why shouldn't we wait for perfect words?
2. What should you be sure about before you write a business pitch, a grant proposal or a speech and why?

● **Simulative Exercise**

Persuade yourself to write something interesting in your life in a leisurely way.

Chapter 12

Blog Writing
博客写作

Abstract
内容概览

Blogging, or writing short entries on a website, can allow you to offer opinions, share ideas, or do independent reporting, but most importantly blogging can help writers have conversations with readers. What makes blogs so different from journalism is the discussion between writer and reader. Blogs can be a forum for writers to get feedback on half–formed ideas and emerging stances, and through comments, readers can talk with and back to writers and build communities. But what draws readers in? The following material will enable you to learn how paying attention to a range of blog elements (including clear headlines, engaging pictures, and distinctive ledes) will help you build an audience.

写博客，或者在网站上编写短小词条，可以让你发表意见、分享想法、或者做独立报道。但最重要的是，写博客可以帮助作者与读者交流。博客与报刊的不同之处在于作者和读者之间可以进行讨论。博客能够成为作家的论坛，使他们得到关于不成熟的想法和新颖立场的反馈。通过评论，读者可以与作家反复交流和创建论坛。但什么才能吸引读者呢？以下内容将使你了解如何注意到一系列能帮助你吸引读者的博客元素（包括清晰的标题、动人的图片、独特的导语）。

Basic Knowledge
基础知识

Introduction

There are a lot of people who have the heart in writing but have not yet found the right avenue to scribble their thoughts and ideas. There are those who have successfully found the perfect avenue but have not yet realized the full potentials of the tool. Making a blog is quite a very simple and easy process to complete. While to some this may look like very complicated like solving an algebraic problem, but generally of people who have tried web logging would say the otherwise. Below are some of the useful tips that one can use in making a web log:

a. Make sure that you know where your skills and knowledge lie. There are a lot of web loggers who have diverse thoughts in their mind that at times they are not able to come up with one solid idea to create. Make sure that you decongest your mind with the topics that you want to write. Write the things that are driving too much passion for you.

b. Make sure that you are able to create a draft before creating a final web log article. Drafting is always advised prior to having a final form because the draft allows you to re-create and re-establish your thoughts and ideas.

c. Choose the best web log application tool. You can choose from using the Blog Spot site or the WordPress application when creating your web log. These two known tools are providing very powerful features that can help you jump start your web logging career.①

简介

很多人都有写作的愿望，但没有找到正确的途径来写下他们的想法和思想。有些人虽然成功地找到了完美途径，但还没有意识到它的全部潜力。其实写博客是一个非常简单和容易完成的过程。但对于某些人来说，这看起来如同代数题般复杂。然而，通常来说，那些尝试写过网络日志的人会持有相反态度。下面是一些可以用来编写网络日志的实用技巧：

---

① Daniel Harris, Blogging100 Success Secrets, Lulu. com, 2008, p. 16.

1. 一定要知道自己拥有哪个方面的知识和技能。很多的网络日志写手的头脑中有各种各样的想法，因此他们常常并不能提出一个可靠的想法来进行创造。确保用你想写的主题来抒发自己的想法，并写下那些你所热忱的事情。

2. 在创建最终网络日志前，一定要打草稿，因为这样可以让你重新创作并重新建立你的想法和思想。

3. 选择最好的网络文章编辑工具。在编辑你的网络日志时，你可以选择 Blog Spot 网站或者 WordPress 软件。这两个工具功能非常强大，可以帮助你在你的网络日志事业的起始阶段突飞猛进。

Writing Requirement

In *The Elements of Blogging: Expanding the Conversation of Journalism,* Mark Leccese and Jerry Lanson dissect blog posts in order to identify and examine their key parts. Below are some of the elements they highlight as well as some examples from local blogs.

Headlines (Titles)

A headline or title not only helps draw in readers' attention with an interesting hook, but by containing keywords that Google and other search engines use, the right headline can bring anyone to your blog. As Leccese and Lanson note, search engines work by creating indexes of the words they find on the web. By using keywords in your headline, there is a greater chance that more browsers will find your blog. Headlines, however, are more than just keywords. They need to be short, 10 words or less, and intriguing.

Ledes

The first sentence of a post should have a conversational tone and articulate the main point of the blog post. Internet readers can easily navigate away from a post, so making your lede interesting and to the point is important.

Images

Pictures not only break up text on a page, but they can also help make your point clearer. Pictures tell stories, but they need to be part of the discussion. Include captions by your images that explain how the image adds to the point you are making.

Links

Links give extra information to your readers. Having links that provide a direct route to information and resources allows your blog to make the most out of being on the web.

Block Quotes

Block quoting gives readers' eyes a break and bolsters the author's credibility. Using a source's words instead rephrasing shows that your points are well supported.

Final Words

Writing a good take–away can, as Leccese and Lanson point out, help readers remember and engage with your post.[①]

写作要求

在《博客写作要素》中，为了鉴别和调查博客文章中的关键部分，马克·雷克萨斯和杰瑞·兰森进行了仔细剖析。以下就是他们重点强调的要素以及一些来自当地博客的范例。

标题（题目）

标题或题目不仅有助于吸引读者的注意力，而且通过包含谷歌或其他搜索引擎使用的关键字，标题可以帮助人们打开你的博客。正如雷克萨斯和兰森提到的，搜索引擎通过它们在网络上找到的单词来进行索引工作。通过在标题中使用关键词，会使更多的浏览器搜到你的博客。然而标题不仅仅只是关键词。它们还需要有趣且简短，最好控制在十个字以内。

导语

文章的第一句话应该有对话式的语气，并能够清晰地表达博文的要点。网络读者可以很容易地离开一个帖子，所以让你的导语有趣非常重要。

图片

图片不仅可以起到在页面上分隔文本的作用，还可以使得你的观点更加清晰。图片可以讲述故事，但是它需要成为你所讨论内容的一部分。你的图片要有说明，以便增强对观点的解释力。

链接

链接可为你的读者提供了额外的信息。链接能够直达相关信息和资源，可以使得你的博客充分享用网络带来的便利。

长段引用

长段引用不但可以让读者的眼睛休息一会，而且还能增强作者的可信度。

---

① Leccese Mark and Jerry Lanson. *The Elements of Blogging: Expanding the Conversation of Journalism*. Focal Press, 2016.

博客写作 | Blog Writing

引用原文而不是改述可以体现出你的观点得到了很好的支持。

结语

如同雷克萨斯和兰森指出的那样，写一个好的结语可以使得你的读者记住并且深刻理解你的文章。

（文献来源：http://www.bakeorbreak.com/）

Analysis

What is most impressive from this blog is those pictures that can show net-surfers a hint what the blog is about. Entitle as "Bake or Break", it clearly conveys to readers that it is the kingdom of baked food. Just notice the style of those pictures. They are uploaded in a high-definition format, which is capable of capturing each detail of the baked food, be it multi-layer cookies, sunflower-shaped cakes or meat-stuffed bread. They project a strong appeal to viewers, propelling them to click their favorite for further reading.

143

Supplementary Readings
拓展阅读

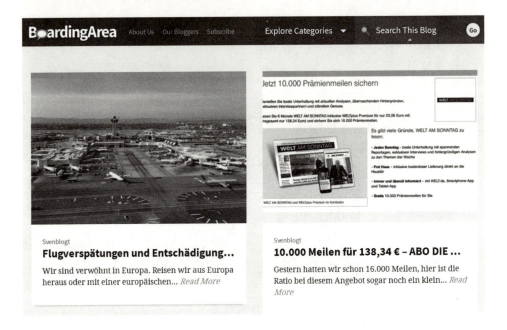

（文献来源：http://boardingarea.com/）

Reading Comprehension

1. What is the theme of this blog?

2. In terms of the title of the blog, what can you learn from it?

3. What's the difference between this blog and the one in Case studies?

● **True or False**

Directions: Read the following sentences and decide whether they are true or false.

1. A lot of web loggers who have diverse thoughts in their mind that at times they are able to come up with one solid idea to create.

博客写作 | Blog Writing

2. The Blog Spot site or the WordPress can help you jump start your web logging career.
3. Writing a good take–away can help readers remember and engage with your post.

● **Gap–Filling**

Directions: Complete each sentence with appropriate words.

1. Blogging, or writing short entries on a website, can allow you to _____, _____, or do _____.
2. Make sure that you know where your _____ and _____.
3. Pictures tell stories, but they need to be part of the _____.

● **Short Answer Questions**

Directions: Answer the following questions briefly.

1. Why should you make a draft before create your final web log article?
2. What is the requirement of headlines (titles) in blog writing?

● **Simulative Exercise**

After reading these instructions, try to design a blog that belongs to your own.

Chapter 13

Short Story
故事写作

Abstract 内容概览

Since prehistoric times, when tales were told around fires and painted on cave walls, stories have been an essential part of our human experience. A short story is simply a tale of events that are linked by cause and effect. It can be true or it can be a work of fiction. We expect stories to have a beginning, middle and end; they involve at least two characters, and some events take place.

For many writers, the short story is the perfect medium. While writing a novel can be a Herculean task, about anybody can craft—and, most importantly, finish—a short story. Like a novel, a good short story will thrill and entertain your reader. With some brainstorming, drafting, and polishing, you can learn how to write a successful short story in no time.

从史前时期以来，人类围着篝火口耳相传那些奇闻逸事并把它们涂画在山洞石壁上，由此，故事成为人类经历的重要一部分。一篇短故事仅仅只是一个由因果关系联系起来的事件，它可以是真实的，也可以是虚构的。我们期望的故事包含有开端、高潮、结尾，以及至少有两个人物和几件事情发生。

对于很多作家来说，短篇小说是最完美的交流媒介。因为写一部长篇小说可能会是一项艰巨的任务，但是几乎任何人都能撰写——最主要的是，能完成——一部短篇小说。跟长篇小说一样，一篇优秀的短篇小说也能让你的读者感到兴奋和快乐。通过集思广益、拟草稿、润色文章，你便能学到如何在短时间内写出一部成功的短篇小说。

故事写作 | Short Story

Basic Knowledge
基础知识

Introduction

A short story is a piece of fiction under 20000 words. More typically, a short story will be 1000 — 5000 words. (Pieces under 1000 words are "short short stories" or "flash fiction", over 20000 and they're novellas.)

Short stories are published in magazines, newspapers and book anthologies. Short stories need:

- A small cast of characters, with one main character;
- A compact time frame, with the story taking place over the course of a few days or weeks;
- A single plot without subplots, though longer short stories may have a subplot.[①]

简介

短篇小说是一篇两万字以内的小说，特别是1000至5000字之内的作品。（1000字以内的称之为小小说或者微型小说，超过20000字为中篇小说。）

短篇小说会经常在杂志、报纸和书刊上发表。一部短篇小说需要具备以下要素：

- 为数不多的几个人物角色，其中只有一个主角。
- 紧凑的时间架构，故事的发生周期为几天或者几周。
- 只有一个主情节，没有其他次要情节，但是稍长的短篇小说也许会有一个次要情节。

Writing Requirement

Step One: Brainstorming Ideas

1. Come up with a plot or scenario. Think about what the story is going to be about and what is going to happen in the story. Consider what you are trying to address or illustrate. Decide what your approach or angle on the story is going to be.

---

① https://www.dailywritingtips.com/story-writing/

2. Focus on a complicated main character. Most short stories will focus on one to two main characters at the most. Think about a main character who has a clear desire, or want, but who is also full of contradictions. Do not simply have a good character or a bad character. Give your main character interesting attributes and feelings so they feel complicated and well-rounded.

3. Create a central conflict for the main character. Every good short story will have a central conflict, where the main character has to deal with an issue or problem. Present a conflict for your main character early in your short story. Make your main character's life difficult or hard.

4. Pick an interesting setting. Another key element of a short story is the setting, or where the events of the story are taking place. You may stick to one central setting for the short story and add details of the setting to scenes with your characters. Choose a setting that is interesting to you, and that you can make interesting for your reader.

5. Think about a particular theme. Many short stories center on a theme and explore it from the point of view of a narrator or main character. You may take a broad theme like "love" "desire" or "loss" and think about it from the point of view of your main character.

6. Plan an emotional climax. Every good short story has a shattering moment where the main character reaches an emotional high point. The climax usually occurs in the last half of the story or close to the end of the story. At the climax of the story, the main character may feel overwhelmed, trapped, desperate, or even out of control.

7. Think of an ending with a twist or surprise. Brainstorm an ending that will leave your reader surprised, shocked, or intrigued. Avoid obvious endings, where the reader can guess the ending before it happens. Give your reader a false sense of security, where they think they know how the story is going to end, and then redirect their attention to another character or an image that leaves them shocked.

Step Two: Creating a First Draft

1. Make a plot outline. Organize your short story into a plot outline with five parts: exposition, an inciting incident, rising action, a climax, falling action, and a resolution. Use the outline as a reference guide as you write the story to ensure it has a clear beginning, middle, and end.

2. Create an engaging opening. Your opening should have action, conflict, or an

unusual image to catch your reader's attention. Introduce the main character and the setting to your reader in the first paragraph. Set your reader up for the key themes and ideas in the story.

3. Stick to one point of view. A short story is usually told in the first person point of view and stays with one point of view only. This helps to give the short story a clear focus and perspective. You can also try writing the short story in third person point of view, though this may create distance between you and your reader.

4. Use dialogue to reveal character and further the plot. The dialogue in your short story should always be doing more than one thing at a time. Make sure the dialogue tells your reader something about the character who is speaking and adds to the overall plot of the story. Include dialogue tags that reveal character and give scenes more tension or conflict.

5. Include sensory details about the setting. Think about how the setting feels, sounds, tastes, smells, and looks to your main character. Describe your setting using the senses so it comes alive for your reader.

6. End with a realization or revelation. The realization or revelation does not have to be major or obvious. It can be subtle, where your characters are beginning to change or see things differently. You can end with a revelation that feels open or a revelation that feels resolved and clear.

Step Three: Polishing the Draft

1. Read the short story out loud. Listen to how each sentence sounds, particularly the dialogue. Notice if the story flows well from paragraph to paragraph. Check for any awkward sentences or phrases and underline them so you can revise them later.

2. Revise the short story for clarity and flow. Most short stories are between 1000 to 7000 words, or one to ten pages long. Be open to cutting scenes or removing sentences to shorten and tighten your story. Make sure you only include details or moments that are absolutely essential to the story you are trying to tell.

3. Come up with an interesting title. Most editors and readers will check the title of the story first to determine if they want to continue reading. Pick a title that will intrigue or interest your reader and encourage them to read the actual story. Use a theme, image or character name from the story as the title.

4. Let others read and critique the short story. Show the short story to friends,

family members and peers at school. Ask them if they find the story emotionally moving and engaging. Be open to constructive criticism from others, as it will only strengthen your story.①

写作要求

第一步：头脑风暴

1. 规划一个主要情节或者故事概要。思考这个故事是关于什么的，将会怎样发生，以及你最想说明和表达的主旨，想清楚你将用什么写作方法和角度来完成这个故事。

2. 锁定一个性格复杂的主角。大部分的短篇小说都会将笔墨用在一个或者最多两个主角身上，主角是拥有明确的理想和追求，但同时性格充满矛盾的人物，切忌只是简单地把主角定位于单纯的好人或坏人。赋予你的主角丰富有趣的性格和情感，这样他们才会成为复杂、完整、圆润的人物。

3. 给主角设定一个主要矛盾。每一篇优秀的短篇小说都会有一个主要矛盾贯穿全文，主角一直在解决这个事件或问题。尽早把主角的主要矛盾表现出来，使主角的生活充满困难和艰辛。

4. 选择一个精彩有趣的场景。写短篇小说另外一个关键要素就是场景的设置，即这个故事将会发生的地点。你应该围绕这一个主要场景展开故事的写作，适当添加一些与人物相关的场景细节。选择一个你感兴趣的场景，只有这样，你才会让故事吸引到读者。

5. 选择一个特定的主旨。很多短篇小说都集中于一个主旨并从故事的讲述者或者主角的角度来阐述它。你可以选择一个范围很广的主旨，比如"爱""理想""失败"，然后再从主角的角度来打磨这篇故事的主旨。

6. 设置一个情感高潮。每一部优秀的短篇小说都会有一个令人震惊的时刻，也就是当主角情感达到最高峰的时候。高潮一般发生在故事的后半部分或者接近尾声的部分。在故事高潮的时候，主角可能会感到不知所措、陷入困境、绝望甚至失去控制。

7. 设置一个意外的转折或者惊喜的结局。一个巧妙的结局会令读者感到惊喜、震惊或者有趣。避免写出平淡无奇的结尾，不要让读者在故事结束之前一眼就猜出结局。先给读者一个虚假的安全感，以为这个故事将会如同他们想象的那样结尾，再出其不意的转移他们的注意力到其他人物和形象身上，最后令

---

① http://www.wikihow.com/Write-a-Short-Story

他们在看到结局时目瞪口呆。

第二步：拟一遍初稿

1. 写出情节提纲。用五部分组成情节梗概：阐述起因、发展、高潮、回落、结局。写作时把提纲当做参考指南使用，就能确保你写出来的故事有一个清楚的脉络，即开端、发展和结尾。

2. 创作一个吸人眼球的开端。开端应该包含行动、矛盾，或者一个非凡的人物形象来达到吸引读者眼球的效果。在第一段中就向读者展示出主角和场景以及主旨和思想。

3. 坚持只用一种人称叙述。通常短篇小说用第一人称的口吻叙述，并且全文只用第一人称，这会使故事重点清晰、观点明确。当然你也可以用第三人称写短故事，但这可能会拉大你和读者之间的距离。

4. 使用对话展现人物形象和推动情节发展。短篇小说中的对话不仅仅是在一个时间只做一件事情。一定要确保你的对话使读者了解到了一些关于说话人的性格和这个故事的主要情节。在对话中要点明说话者，以便展现人物性格，使情节更具紧张感和冲突性。

5. 在场景中添加感性细节。思考一下怎样能使你写的场景为主角所感知、倾听、品尝、嗅闻和打量。用感官体验来描述情节会使故事栩栩如生。

6. 以揭示或启示的手法结尾。揭示和启示不需要占据故事的主体，也不需要明显体现出来，它可以是微妙的，比如人物开始有了变化或者从不同的角度看待事情。你可以尝试以一个开放性的启示结尾，或以一个清晰的、有定论的启示结尾。

第三步：润色草稿

1. 大声读出你写的这篇故事。听听所读的每一句语言，特别是对话。注意段落之间是否衔接自然，找出所有生涩的句子和短语，把它们下画线标记出来以方便后面的改正。

2. 修改文章使其语言更清晰流畅。大部分的短篇小说都在1000至7000字之间，大概一页至十页纸的长度，大胆地删减一些不必要的情节和句子，使你的短故事更加简洁紧凑。一定要保证你所保留的细节和情节对你所阐释的故事是十分有必要的。

3. 拟定一个吸引人的题目。大多数的编辑和读者都会先看题目是否有趣再决定是否继续读下去。选择一个好标题会提起读者的兴趣，激励他们读完整篇故事。可以使用故事的主旨、意象或者人物的名字作为短篇小说的题目。

4. 让其他人阅读并评论你的短篇小说。给朋友、家人、同学展示你的文章，询问他们这篇故事是否令他们感动和入迷。虚心接受别人建设性的批评和建议，因为这会帮助完善你的故事写作。

Case Studies
案例分析

Sample Short Literary Story

Donny smoothed his hands over his suit for the millionth time. The cigarette was almost gone. He'd have to go in soon.

It killed him. It had killed him when he got the call about the funeral. Killed him on the flight there. Killed him while he waited for the single bag he packed for his short stay in Indiana. Killed him as the rental car rumbled up streets he hadn't seen in a decade but knew like the back of his hand.

He could handle the body, he supposed. Some forgotten cousin. A sad thing, but nothing worth coming home over—had one's father not twisted one's arm, financially speaking. Work out west was hard to find. The old man was rich. It was a natural arrangement, of course—none of the thirty somethings he knew could survive out there without accomplished parents—but not one without its inconveniences.

"You got this, Donny. " He checked his reflection in a corner of the window and decided to do away with the sunglasses. "Big tears. Big tears. Big tears. "

They came pretty easily. He'd do the head-down thing, for sure, the *sorry-for-not-staying-dad-I'm-on-a-filming-schedule* thing too. His dad would never ask when he could see Donny's latest appearance, because he was too smart and too caring to ask difficult questions. But the understanding would be there, staring Donny in the face every time he cashed another check.

"You got this. "

He still couldn't make himself walk towards the door.

Here he was, a *professional friggin' actor*, and he couldn't whip up some tears at a family member's funeral. He smashed his fists against his thigh. The extra pain provided by the Indiana cold gave him an idea. He brought his right

故事写作 | Short Story

> hand up, pulled himself out of the window's view, and slapped himself in the face. Hard. Again.
>
> The tears flowed easily, then.
>
> Into the funeral home. His cheeks still stung from the slaps. His tears made it worse. He felt like a gigantic idiot. The family, or the few that remained this far into the service, all turned from their front row seats to look.
>
> None of their smiles looked real. He returned one just as fake.
>
> Then, dad stood. Richard Bolt, the brake king of the Midwest, receiving his actor son back home. He didn't raise his arms for a hug, so Donny lowered his.
>
> Three more steps. Two more. One. Still no arms. No smile, either. Only a quick admonition before he turned:
>
> "Your cheek is red."

（文献来源：http://www.wikihow.com/Sample/Short-Literary-Story）

Analysis

This short story is excellent because it narrates a main character with very notable personality, plus a story line full of twists and turns. The ending part takes the reader by surprise, for it is totally out of their expectations. The story, about 500 words, shows us the careful arrangement and calculation of words in each part of its plot. From the very beginning to the end, we can hardly point out one single sentence that seems redundant. Another feature of the story lies in its language style, which is informal, colloquial and abundant in short sentences. In this way, it'll get closer to people's life and render the story more rhythmic tensions, which is more appealing and pleasurable for reading.

Supplementary Readings
拓展阅读

Sample Short Love Story

It was very hard for Sam to keep from screaming at the unfairness of it all.

She had been working at the newspaper for years. She wasn't always the best writer, and she certainly could have been a bit more social with the rest of the office staff, but she was good at her job, and she had become invaluable to the editor. Derek had always valued her opinion for what it was, and he trusted her more than anyone else at the paper.

But that was before Christine.

Christine slammed into the newsroom like a Category 5 hurricane. She tore down everything Sam had worked so hard to build and left a trail of destruction in her wake. Within her first month, she'd managed to get four good reporters fired, and at least a few others were on the chopping block.

And Derek seemed to love her immediately.

It didn't matter to him that Sam had given the paper everything or that he used to trust her implicitly. When Christine winked, complimented him, and broke things off with her fiancé to "get to know him better", all of that went out the window. It was like Caesar and Cleopatra all over again.

She demanded Sam's resignation two weeks later.

It was sheer luck that Christine wasn't in a position to influence hiring. No matter how much she complained about Sam's work, she couldn't get her way.

And then came the last straw: Derek promoted Christine to the job Sam had been promised, and that was it. A carefully crafted letter of resignation made its way to her direct supervisor's desk.

Truth be told, Sam still wasn't sure whether it was the right decision. But she'd given her two weeks' notice, and her desk would have to be cleared out by then. She had to focus on that.

When she walked back into the office that Wednesday night, there he was.

She had hoped that today would be the day he'd decide he didn't have to work until all hours and let her clear out her desk in peace. But Derek, who always seemed to have a sixth sense about her, picked his head up the second she made it across the room.

There wasn't much left: a calendar, a mug, a few notebooks, and a well-worn chemistry textbook lined the box she brought for her things. He at least had the decency to let her finish packing before calling her over.

This wasn't going to end well, and she knew it.

"Are you okay?" he asked once she was settled into the uncomfortable chair across from him. She nodded mutely, and he cleared his throat.

"Good. I, uh…you'll have to forgive the lack of professionalism here, but…"

She tilted her head. "But what?" she asked graciously, wondering briefly if he knew how thin a line he was treading. His eyes fixed on her, and it was like she was seeing the Derek of three months ago. She couldn't breathe.

"Please don't go," he blurted. She blinked, working hard to keep face blank. He leaned over the desk theatrically, and it was hard for Sam to keep from smiling. Whenever he pulled that move, she couldn't help but think Derek looked a bit like Cary Grant.

"I don't know why you're leaving, but we need you here. You're the best writer at the paper. And I need your advice. Please stay. "

And there he was, giving her that look again—the one that always got him an extra slice of cake at company gatherings, could probably get him out of prison, and was very effective at melting a reporter's heart. Sam felt her reasons for leaving start drifting away. He needed her. And she had always been there for him. How could she leave?

She felt the corners of her mouth turning up and forced them back down again. No way could she cave now; she was right in the middle of packing up her stuff! "What about Christine?"

Derek shook his head, sighing audibly. "Christine is…well, she's something, all right. " He locked his eyes on hers, and Sam felt herself unable to look away. "But you have something that she just doesn't. "

Sam furrowed her brow. "And what might that be?"

He ran a hand through his hair (his beautiful, perfect, full head of hair, Sam thought in spite of herself), seemingly struggling for words. She waited, biting her lip in anticipation.

Finally he spoke. "You're kind. You're funny. You're incredibly talented but so modest that hardly anyone knows how amazing you are, even though they should. You keep to yourself, but you're easy to talk to, and I know you'll be honest with me no matter what I ask. Basically, you're one of very few people I look forward to seeing every day, and I would genuinely hate to see you go." By the end of his soliloquy, his face had gone red, and Sam noticed that he was twisting his tie around in his hands—almost as if she were making him nervous.

She smiled at the thought. And then she had an idea that was so crazy and out of character for her she couldn't believe it could have come out of her own rational, analytical brain. But this is my last chance, really, she realized. If I don't do this now, I'll never be able to.

So she blurted it out before she had too much time to convince herself it was a horrible idea.

"If you'd hate it so much, prove it to me. Take me to dinner tonight. You can give me more compliments," she laughed, "and reasons you want me to stay."

He opened his mouth, his lips forming the word "no", then caught her eye again and shut his mouth. Sam's breath was stuck in her throat. She stared at him, refusing to blink, until at last she heard the words she hadn't known she was waiting for.

"You know what? It's a date."

（文献来源：http://www.wikihow.com/Sample/Short-Love-Story）

Reading Comprehension

Study three main steps above and discuss with a partner whether there is anything else that you think is good and useful for writing a short story.

故事写作 | Short Story

Exercise 课后练习

● **True or False**

Directions: Read the following sentences and decide whether they are true or false.

1. A short story should involve no less than two major characters, and some events take place.
2. A short story had better contains a single plot with multiple subplots, which enrich and liven up the scenarios of the short story.
3. The title is not as important as the contents of the short story.

● **Gap–Filling**

Directions: Complete each sentence with appropriate words.

1. Do not simply have a good character or a bad character. Give your main character interesting attributes and feelings so they feel _____ and _____.
2. Organize your short story into a plot outline with five parts: _____, _____, _____, _____, and _____.

● **Short Answer Questions**

Directions: Answer the following questions briefly.

1. What're the three steps of Writing Requirements of a short story?
2. How can we come up with a successful ending in short story writing?

● **Simulative Exercise**

　　Based on your understanding and learning of the methods of short stories writing, what's the most typical weakness of your short stories writing formerly and how do you plan to improve that?

Keys
参考答案

Chapter 1　Academic Writing Style / 学术写作概述

● True or False

T F T

● Gap-Filling

1. sexist language

2. passive verbs; doer

3. qualifying adverbs; overgeneralizations

● Short Answer Questions

1. It teaches students to analyze; it allows students to convey their understanding; it has a strong focus on technique and style; it teaches students to think critically and objectively.

2. Use passive verbs to avoid stating the "doer".

● Simulative Exercise

Omitted.

Chapter 2　Essay / 论文

● True or False

F F T

● Gap-Filling

1. lawyer; persuade; convince

2. opinion; logical

● Short Answer Questions

1. It is normally difficult to come up a thesis statement early on, so it's always good

to read up on the assignment question and make notes on relevant concepts, theories, and studies first.

2. First, you should review the content of the essay. Second, you should pay attention to the questions related to the structure and flow. Third, look over your use of outside sources.

● Simulative Exercise

Omitted.

Chapter 3　Literature Review and Book Review / 文献综述和书评

● True or False

F T F

● Gap-Filling

1. The Literature; Literature Review

2. answers; review

● Short Answer Questions

1. First, what others have done or what you did in a previous paper.

   Second, the downside or limit of what they did or why you decided to further the work you did in a previous paper.

   Third, your solution or improvement.

2. A book review should include a description of the scope and organization of the book. Besides, it should also encompass the evaluation of how successful the book is in its aims.

● Simulative Exercise

Omitted.

Chapter 4　Application Essay / 申请书

● True or False

F F T

● Gap-Filling

1. personal story; highlight

2. details; examples; reasons

3. proofreading

● Short Answer Questions

1. The number one piece of advice is "Be yourself", and number two is "Start early."
2. Because it will make your application likes a resume, and can't show any detail about yourself.

● Simulative Exercise

Omitted.

Chapter 5　Resume and CV / 简历和履历

● True or False

T F F

● Gap-Filling

1. name; phone number; address; email
2. teaching; research; administrative

● Short Answer Questions

1. Resume is to present the case that your experience and skills make you a great candidate for a particular position while CV's purpose is focus on academic experience and accomplishments for an academic position.

   Resume's audience is any possible employer or HR employee while CV's is fellow academics on a hiring committee.

   Resume's length is probably only 1 page and absolutely no longer than 2 pages, but CV's is much longer with less limitations of length.

   Resume's description of experience is focused on active skills linked with quantifiable results you've achieved. But CV is not often needed.

2. Include your job title, your employer, the time span you worked, and the location where you worked. Use your active verbs and keywords to describe work experience in bullet points with two to three bullets under each job. Use present tense verbs for current jobs and past tense verbs for past jobs.

● Simulative Exercise

Omitted.

Chapter 6　Note Making / 笔记

● True or False

T F F

● Gap-Filling

1. abbreviated; compressed

2. logical; memorable

● Short Answer Questions

1. Use abbreviations, initials, and shortened forms of commonly used terms. Don't attempt to write continuous prose.

2. Five steps:

　　Label and file your notes (physically or online).

　　Cross reference them with any handouts.

　　Read through your notes and fill in any details from your additional reading or research.

　　Link new information to what you already know.

　　Discuss with others, compare, fill in gaps.

● Simulative Exercise

Omitted.

Chapter 7　Business Writing Style / 商务写作概述

● True or False

F T F

● Gap-Filling

1. professional; comprehensive; informative

2. eliminates; identify

● Short Answer Questions

1. Business writing skills can foster effective communication, boost credibility, help to keep records, and create opportunities

2. We need to pay much attention to clear purpose, clarity and conciseness, awareness of audience, appropriate tone and attention to form.

● Simulative Exercise

Omitted.

Chapter 8　Memo / 备忘录

● True or False

T F F

● Gap-Filling

1. the event; circumstance; background

2. your findings; detailed information

3. business writing

● Short Answer Questions

1. They bring attention to problems and they solve problems.

2. You need to skip a line between sentences.

● Simulative Exercise

Omitted.

Chapter 9　Business Letters / 商务信函

● True or False

T F F

● Gap-Filling

1. exchange business related information

2. 8/7; Sender's Address, Date, Inside Address, Salutation, Body, Closing, (Typist initials), and Enclosures

● Short Answer Questions

1. The business letter can be used to build goodwill, make a last impression, build and maintain business relation, exchange business information to name but a few. It can also be used as records and references, even an authoritative proof.

2. Invitation letter, thank-you letter, appology letter, etc.

● Simulative Exercise

Omitted.

Chapter 10　Business Report / 商业报告

● True or False

T F F

● Gap-Filling

1. background; context; approach; methodology

2. Literature Review; peer-reviewed; literature

● Short Answer Questions

1. The key to a good report is in-depth analysis. Good writers will show their reader how they have interpreted their findings.

2. A business report should contain the following parts: Title Page, Table of Contents, Executive summary, Introduction, Literature, Review, Method, Findings, Recommendations, Conclusion, References and Appendices.

● Simulative Exercise

Omitted.

Chapter 11　Leisure Writing Style / 休闲写作概述

● True or False

F T F

● Gap-Filling

1. generating; ideas.

2. confused; Condense; organized.

● Short Answer Questions

1. First, if you just stop to wait for a perfect word, your writing may never begin or continue. Second, if you just wait instead of start writing, you will probably let go of the notion of immediate perfection. Third, once you have started, you can go back and revise what you have.

2. You should do enough research and condense the main nugget of your points into a short sentence so that you know precisely what you mean to communicate and compose a tight, organized piece.

● Simulative Exercise

Omitted.

Chapter 12　　Blog Writing / 博客写作

● True or False

F T T

● Gap-Filling

1. offer opinions; share ideas; independent reporting

2. skills; knowledge lie

3. discussion

● Short Answer Questions

1. Drafting is always advised prior to having a final form because the draft allows you to re-create and re-establish your thoughts and ideas.

2. They need keywords, be short, 10 words or less, and intriguing.

● Simulative Exercise

Omitted.

Chapter 13　　Short Story / 故事写作

● True or False

F F F

● Gap-Filling

1. complicated; well-rounded

2. an inciting incident; rising action; a climax; falling action; a resolution

● Short Answer Questions

1. Step one: brainstorming ideas; step two: creating a first draft; step three: polishing the draft.

2. Think of an ending with a twist or surprise. Brainstorm an ending that will leave your reader surprised, shocked, or intrigued. Avoid obvious endings.
　　End with a realization or revelation.

● Simulative Exercise

Omitted.

References
参考文献

英文书目

Bailey Jr, Edward P. *The Plain English Approach to Business Writing*. Oxford: Oxford University Press, 1997.

Bailey, Stephen, *Academic Writing: A Handbook for International Students*. New York: Routledge, 2015.

Bargiela-Chiappini, Francesca, and Catherine Ross Nickerson. *Writing Business: Genres, Media and Discourses*. London: Routledge, 2014.

Bottomley, Jane, *Academic Writing for International Students of Science*. London: Routledge, 2014.

Bowman, J. P. and B. P. Branchaw, *Business Report Writing*, 2nd ed. Chicago: The Dryden Press, 1988

Guffey, Rhodes and Rogin, *Business Communication: Process and Product*, Third Brief Canadian Edition. Thomson-Nelson, 2010

Johnson, Roy, *Revision and Examinations: Guidance Notes for Students*. Manchester: Clifton Press, 1993

Kahneman, Daniel, *Thinking, Fast and Slow*. London: Macmillan, 2011.

Mark, Leccese and Jerry Lanson, *The Elements of Blogging: Expanding the Conversation of Journalism*. London: Focal Press, 2016.

McGinty, S. M., *The College Application Essay*. New York: College Board, 2015.

Montero, Marcus, *Atlantic Crossing: A Comparison of European and American Society*. York: York University Press, 2008.

Nourse, K. A, *How to Write College Application Essay*, New York: McGraw-Hill Companies, 2001.

Ravelli, Louise, and Robert A. Ellis, eds, *Analysing Academic Writing: Contextualized*

Frameworks. London: A&C Black, 2005.

Spilka, Rachel, ed, *Writing in the Workplace: New Research Perspectives*. London: SIU Press, 1998.

Swales, John M., and Christine B. Feak., *Academic Writing for Graduate Students: Essential Tasks and Skills*. Vol. 1. Ann Arbor, MI: University of Michigan Press, 2004.

Tanabe, Gen, and Kelly Tanabe, *50 Successful Ivy League Application Essays*. London: Super College, 2015.

Wallwork, Adrian, *English for Writing Research Papers*. New York: Springer, 2016.

中文书目

陈明瑶，陈文娟编著：《英语实用写作与学术写作》，浙江工商大学出版社，2011 年。

陈亚丽著：《英文商务写作：案例分析与实践》，天津大学出版社，2004 年。

范红等编：《英文商务写作教程》，清华大学出版社，2000 年。

高桂珍，金敬红主编：《任务型学术写作》，中国人民大学出版社，2008 年。

李晓文，刘晓辉编著：《英语学术写作：传播科学的媒介》，机械工业出版社，2011 年。

英文网站

http://library.bcu.ac.uk/learner

http://owll.massey.ac.nz/assignment-types

http://www.ets.org/gre/revised_general/prepare/analytical_writing/issue/sample_responses

http://www.library.unimelb.edu.au/libraries/bee.

http://www.mytopbusinessideas.com/why-writing-skills-important/

http://www.law.cuny.edu/legal-writing/students/memorandum/memorandum-3.html.

http://www.studymode.com/essays/Mother-Teresa-38974231.html

http://www.wikihow.com

http://www.writinghelp-central.com

https://chrisgrundemann.com/index.php/2012/creative-writing-fun-profit/

https://ewritingservice.com/blog/what-is-the-importance-of-academic-writing-for-a-student/

https://jamaicagleaner.com/article/art-leisure/20170115/whats-your-motivation-start-writing

https://owl.english.purdue.edu

https://oup.useremarkable.com/production/images/uploads/3676/original/sample_Business_Report.pdf?1479137052.

https://writing.wisc.edu/Handbook

https://www.academia.edu/4607842/Summary_Writing_GUIDELINES

https://www.adelaide.edu.au/.../learningGuide_BusinessReportWriting.pdf

https://www.buzzle.com/articles/business-report-example.html.

https://www.dailywritingtips.com/story-writing/

https://www.entrepreneur.com/article/233264

https://www.kent.ac.uk/learning/resources/studyguides/notemaking.pdf.

https://www.pinterest.com/pin/207376757812964611/

https://www.thebalance.com/functional-resume-example-2063203

https://www.umuc.edu/current-students/learningresources/writing-center/writing-resources/memos/